THE DARK SIDE OF DHARMA

THE DARK SIDE OF DHARMA
Meditation, Madness and other Maladies on the Contemplative Path

Anna Lutkajtis

AEON

First published in 2020 by
Aeon Books Ltd
PO Box 76401
London W5 9RG

Copyright © 2020 by Anna Lutkajtis

The right of Anna Lutkajtis to be identified as the author of this work has been asserted in accordance with §§ 77 and 78 of the Copyright Design and Patents Act 1988.

All rights reserved. No part of this publication may be reproduced, stored in a retrieval system, or transmitted, in any form or by any means, electronic, mechanical, photocopying, recording, or otherwise, without the prior written permission of the publisher.

British Library Cataloguing in Publication Data

A C.I.P. for this book is available from the British Library

ISBN-13: 978-1-91350-459-5

Typeset by Medlar Publishing Solutions Pvt Ltd, India
Printed in Great Britain

www.aeonbooks.co.uk

For Ricardo Claudio Farago
(and Maya and Zen)

AUTHOR BIOGRAPHY

Anna Lutkajtis is a postgraduate researcher from Sydney, Australia. Her research focuses on mysticism, the dark night of the soul and the healing potential of altered states of consciousness. She is particularly interested in the relationship between mental illness and spirituality, mystical experiences, and how techniques that were originally designed for contemplative purposes have been integrated into modern Western psychology. Her Masters thesis, "The Dark Side of Dharma", examined why the adverse effects of meditation, whilst well-known in spiritual and religious traditions, have been ignored in contemporary Western secular contexts. She holds a B. Psychology (Hons) degree from UNSW Sydney, a Master of Art Administration degree from UNSW Sydney, and a Master of Arts (Research: Religion Studies) degree from The University of Sydney. Her publications can be found at www.annalutkajtis.com.

COVER ARTWORK "WHEEL OF LIFE" BY MAN BAHADUR DONG

For centuries, *thangkas* have been an important teaching tool for the transmission of the words and visions of the Buddha. Drawn and painted with mineral colours on cotton or silk cloth, these delicate paintings depict either a deity or the life events of Shakyamuni Buddha, the founder of the Buddhist tradition. To this day, in Tibetan Buddhism, these images are used by Dharma practitioners to support their visualisation practice.

The artist, Man Bahadur Dong, received his first lessons in *thangka* painting from his uncle at the age of fifteen. He has been practising as an independent *thangka* painter in Kathmandu, Nepal, for the past twelve years and is skilled in all types of *thangka* styles. During this time he has refined his work through his study of the tantric texts that describe the deities he paints.

Man Bahadur Dong's work is available to view and purchase here:

Website: https://sites.google.com/site/kavrethangkaart/home
Facebook: @KavreeThangkaArt
Instagram: @kavreethangkaart
Email: kalsangtenzin79@yahoo.com

CONTENTS

ACKNOWLEDGEMENTS	xv
PREFACE	xvii

CHAPTER ONE
A brief history of meditation: east and west   1
    What is meditation?   1
    Hindu approaches to meditation   3
    Buddhist approaches to meditation   6
    Meditation in the west: mainstream   9
    Meditation in the west: clinical   17

CHAPTER TWO
The dark side of dharma: meditation adverse effects
and the "dark night"   21
    The meditation backlash   21
    The dark night of the soul   23
    The *dukkha nanas*   25
    Insight gone wrong   28
    "Adverse effects" in meditation research   32
    The dark night project   38

CHAPTER THREE
From enlightenment to symptom relief and personal
   transformation   43
  Meditation as a western therapeutic intervention   43
  Meditation as a panacea   44
  The relaxation response   49
  Issues of self and non-self   52
  Mourning the loss of the self   56
  Meditation research methods   59

CHAPTER FOUR
Making meditation secular: meditation as a detachable
   technique   63
  "Secular" meditation   63
  Meditation as a detachable technique   65
  De-contextualisation: privileging meditation
    and marginalising religious context   66
  Simplification: psychological, pathological
    and neural reductionism   71
  Re-contextualisation: "the buddha was a scientist"
    and the creation of a western meditation lineage   74

CHAPTER FIVE
Meditation divorced from religion   79
  Meditation adverse effects in religious traditions   79
  Preparation   84
  Supportive context   88
  Teacher and technique   91
  Individual differences and psychopathology   97

CHAPTER SIX
"The answer to all your problems?" meditation
  and the media   101
  All good news stories   101
  Meditation tropes   103
  Scientist-journalist communication   105
  Celebrity gurus and celebrity meditators   109
  Meditation for sale   111
  How should meditation be portrayed?   115

CHAPTER SEVEN
Facing the shadow 117
    The denial of the dark side 117
    Spiritual bypassing 119
    The future 123

REFERENCES 131
INDEX 151

ACKNOWLEDGEMENTS

To the many people who have made this book possible, I am truly grateful.

The existence of this book owes much to the mentorship of Professor Carole M. Cusack. Thank you for allowing a serendipitous phone enquiry to result in this research project and book.

Many thanks are owed to Daniel M. Ingram, for being relentlessly transparent in his dealings with the dharma and for helping me through my own dark night of the soul. Daniel is one of the rare people I have encountered who are willing to talk about the dark side of dharma with absolute openness.

Finally, thank you to all my fellow academics, meditators, consciousness explorers and seekers (in particular Bart Pawlik and Giovanni Dienstmann). Your work, your lived experiences, and your enlightening conversations provide an unending source of inspiration.

Several of the chapters from this book have been published in peer-reviewed academic journals, and I am grateful to the publishers for their permission to reprint these articles here as chapters. These articles have been edited to varying degrees, and sections have been removed to avoid repetition between chapters, but the main body of the paper remains. Thank you to Douglas Ezzy and the editors at the *Journal for the Academic Study of Religion*. Thank you also to Carole M. Cusack and the editors at *Literature & Aesthetics*. The original articles are listed here:

Chapter 2.
Lutkajtis, Anna. Delineating the Dark Night in Buddhist Postmodernism. *Literature & Aesthetics*, vol. 29, no. 2 (2019).

Chapter 3.
Lutkajtis, Anna. The Dark Side of Dharma: Why Have Adverse Effects of Meditation Been Ignored in Contemporary Western Secular Contexts? *Journal for the Academic Study of Religion*, vol. 31, no. 2 (2018).

Chapter 6.
Lutkajtis, Anna. "The Answer to All Your Problems?" The Overly Positive Presentation of Meditation in the Media. *Journal for the Academic Study of Religion*, vol. 32, no. 1 (2019).

Finally, this book is for Ricardo Farago—your unconditional love, belief, and support made this work possible.

PREFACE

I first learned to meditate in 2011. Like many people, I came to the practice for non-religious reasons: stress relief and the myriad health and wellbeing benefits that were promised. I did not know exactly what meditation was or where it came from, only that it was "ancient" and associated with Eastern religions and gurus. I took a short course, learned a basic technique and diligently practised at least once per day as the teacher instructed. During the first week of my meditation practice I experienced strong headaches after each session. I thought this was unusual and checked in with my teacher, who assured me this was normal for some people and would pass after the first week or so (they did). I continued to meditate, and noticed another strange effect. Every time I would begin my practice, within several minutes I would feel myself drop into a trance-like state and I would see a purple sphere of light appear in the centre of my vision. This light was not at all unpleasant, but it was unusual and I was curious as to whether it meant something. Again, I asked my teacher. It was nothing, he said. Some people see lights when they meditate, others hear sounds. None of it mattered, just keep going.

To me, this was a highly unsatisfying answer, so of course I went straight to Google and typed in "purple light when meditating."

After some basic searching I seemed to have an answer—the light appeared to be a *nimitta*. The Pali word *nimitta* literally means "sign" and the *nimitta* itself is a mind-generated object that appears when a meditator has reached a good state of concentration. Immediately I was both intrigued and annoyed—either my meditation teacher did not know what a *nimitta* was (which was concerning, given his self-professed status as a "meditation expert" and the high cost of his meditation course), or he was concealing this information from me. Either way, I wanted to know why.

The experience with the *nimitta* was the first of a number of strange and unusual experiences that I went on to have while meditating. These experiences piqued my curiosity to such a degree that I decided to pursue postgraduate research in this area. In particular, I wanted to investigate a meditation-related phenomenon that I was regularly encountering in my personal conversations with other meditators, but which very few people were talking about openly—meditation side effects or "adverse effects." It seemed that many meditators, especially those with serious disciplined practices, were experiencing meditation adverse effects. For some, these effects were completely unexpected and undesirable. Others believed that meditation adverse effects were a normal part of the contemplative path, and as such they were a welcome sign of progress. There were various names that meditators gave to meditation adverse effects, including the *dukkha nanas*, kundalini crisis, and the "dark night."

My curiosity regarding meditation adverse effects eventually led me to the Religion Studies department at the University of Sydney, Australia. After a serendipitous phone call with Professor Carole Cusack, I ended up enrolling in a Master of Arts (Research) degree in Religion Studies. My thesis was titled *The Dark Side of Dharma: Why Have Adverse Effects of Meditation Been Ignored in Contemporary Western Secular Contexts?* Through my academic research I discovered that while the scientific studies and popular media coverage of meditation have been overwhelmingly positive, a small but growing number of studies also speak of meditation adverse effects. A close examination of the scientific literature revealed that adverse effects were described even in early meditation research. These effects included profound but de-stabilising insights, problematic spiritual emergencies, and the exacerbation of pre-existing mental health conditions. What I found particularly fascinating was that in religious traditions, such as Buddhism, these types of difficulties associated with meditation are acknowledged, and are usually understood to be either milestones on the path to enlightenment, the result of improper practice, or due to individual differences. Further, in traditional contexts, meditation teachers are equipped to deal with adverse effects when they arise. However, in modern Western secular contexts, negative effects associated with meditation have largely been overlooked or ignored in both the academic literature and in the popular media. Again, I wanted to know *why*.

During the course of my research project I became a more critical and analytical consumer of information about meditation. One of the first things I discovered is that it really does not make sense to talk about "Buddhist meditation" or "Hindu meditation"—rather, there are hundreds, possibly thousands, of different meditation techniques that derive from various religious sects and lineages. These techniques are heavily embedded within the specific contexts of particular traditions. I quickly learned about the rather short history of Eastern meditation in the West, and how a small number of meditation practices have been appropriated from religious traditions, "secularised" and incorporated into Western psychology and medicine. I also discovered that there is no definitive boundary that separates "secular" meditation from "religious" meditation. In fact, some modern, Eastern-derived meditation practices and Western psychotherapies have co-arisen and been mutually informed by one another, making them very difficult, if not impossible, to separate.

My thesis argued that meditation adverse effects have been ignored in Western secular settings mainly due to three factors. Firstly, in contemporary Western society the goal of meditation has shifted from a religious goal (enlightenment) to a psychological goal (symptom relief and personal transformation), leading to the assumption that meditation is harmless and "good for everyone." Secondly, popular "secular" meditation techniques have been decontextualised and divorced from the religious literature and contemplative practitioners who could shed light on possible difficulties associated with meditation. Finally, the image of meditation that is portrayed by the popular media is radically simplified and overwhelmingly positive, to the point that meditation has been depicted as a type of panacea or "cure all."

The fact that meditation adverse effects have been under-researched and overlooked has significant implications given the current popularity of meditation practices in a large variety of non-traditional settings, including therapy, education, and the workplace. Meditation teaching is an unregulated industry, meaning that there are an unaccounted-for number of teachers who practise independently, possibly without any awareness of potential contraindications or adverse effects. Further, people now self-refer to meditation via the internet and seek meditation in highly variable settings outside of clinical programs, for example, in the form of performance improvement services such as coaching, or apps. Given the current popularity and proliferation of secular meditation-related products and services, it is important to understand why, in the modern West, meditation adverse effects have been overlooked, under-researched, and generally misunderstood. This book, which is based on my Master's thesis research, attempts to answer that question.

Anna Lutkajtis 2020

CHAPTER ONE

A brief history of meditation: east and west

> *The attempt to abstract out the primary characteristics of meditation from a grab bag of traditions in order to come to some purified essence or generic definition is a uniquely Western and relatively recent phenomenon. This tendency should be considered, however powerful and convincing its claim as an objective, universal, and value-free method, to be an artifact of one culture attempting to comprehend another that is completely different.*
>
> —Eugene Taylor.[1]

What is meditation?

The practice of meditation is found in most, if not all, of the world's major religious traditions. Ancient traditions throughout the world have used meditation as a technique to go beyond conscious thought and to experience the inner depths of the mind. Meditation is found in Christianity (in the form of contemplation), Hinduism (from which

---

[1] Eugene Taylor, "Introduction" in Murphy, M. and Donovan, S. *The Physical and Psychological Effects of Meditation: A Review of Contemporary Research with a Comprehensive Bibliography 1931–1996*. CA: Institute of Noetic Sciences, 1999: 2.

Transcendental Meditation is derived), Buddhism (from which mindfulness and *vipassana* meditation originated), Judaism and Islam. Religious texts describe many meditation techniques that range from sitting quietly (such as Buddhist concentration practices) to physical movement of the body (such as Hindu-derived Hatha Yoga) or scriptural reading and prayer (such as in the Christian practice of *lectio divina*). Approaches to meditation also differ based on the object of meditation (for example, a concrete object versus more abstract thoughts, feelings, images, or qualities such as compassion or peace), type of attention cultivated (for example, focused attention versus open monitoring), cognitive processes involved (simply observing thoughts versus deliberately modifying them) and the desired outcome or goal (for example, a state of calm versus a state of excitation). The *Vigyan Bhairav Tantra* is a single text that describes over one hundred different meditation methods, including silent sitting, breath observation, mental imagery, vigorous chaotic breathing, intense activity and sexual excitation (Awasthi 2013). Hence, defining meditation is difficult and there is often disagreement regarding what type of practices constitute meditation. For example, movement-based practices such as yoga, qigong and tai chi may be considered a form of meditation by some, while others define meditation in a stricter sense to refer only to internal mental practices that focus on attention and concentration.

It is also important to note that within religions, meditation techniques are culturally embedded within very specific contexts. Religious studies scholar Ann Taves (2009: 81) notes that religious traditions that include meditation practices have "created data of various sorts, including philosophical discussions of meditation, rituals that include meditation, and, especially in the modern era, post hoc accounts of experiences that occurred during meditation."

Therefore, to simply refer to "Christian meditation" or "Buddhist meditation" is not very meaningful, as both religions contain a vast range of different philosophies, traditions and lineages. As such, meditation practices are best understood within the context of certain schools of thought, individual teachers and specific texts. Hence, this book will, where possible, attempt to distinguish between specific types of meditation techniques.

In Eastern religions such as Buddhism, meditation practice has continued unbroken over centuries. In the West, however, the living tradition of meditation largely disappeared with the destruction of classical civilisation (although the Eastern Orthodox churches have a rich and varied contemplative tradition), and interest in meditation only began to gain mainstream traction in the West when Eastern meditative practices were reintroduced by Asian meditation teachers. As such, the main meditation techniques that are practiced in the modern West today derive from Hindu and Buddhist traditions.

Hindu approaches to meditation

Defining Hinduism is difficult. As Klaus Klostermaier (2007: 15) notes: "The long history, the vastness and the heterogeneity of Hinduism offer enormous challenges to each and every description of the tradition." The terms "Hinduism" and "Hindu" were created by outsiders in colonial times in order to more easily explain and translate India's religious and social life. While there were many localised religions throughout India, categorising them as just one strand of religious thought made it easier for outsiders to understand. As a result, some scholars argue that the term "Hinduism" covers such a diversity of traditions that it has no meaning. However, for the purposes of this book, the most useful way to define Hinduism is as an umbrella term for all the traditions that adhere to the sacred scriptures of the *Vedas*: ancient Indian texts in Sanskrit that cover psychology, religion, and philosophy, and that date back to approximately 3500 B.C.E. In Indian languages, the preferred description of Hinduism is *Vaidika dharma*, the "Vedic Law" (Klostermaier 2007: 15).

The *Vedas*, the *Upanishads* (c. 800–600 B.C.E.), the *Bhagavad Gita* (c. 500–300 B.C.E.), and the *Yoga Sutras* (c. 200 B.C.E.–300 C.E.), are the major source texts regarding Hindu forms of meditation. These scriptures contain references to meditation practices embedded within a religious and philosophical context that addresses issues such as ethics, prescriptions for living, and theories regarding the existence of God. In Hinduism, the distinction between philosophy and religion is not as clear-cut as it is in contemporary Western culture. The concept of "religion" is captured by the Sanskrit word *dharma*, which can be translated as "law," and Hindu religion is referred to as *sanâtana-dharma* (eternal law) (Feuerstein 2008: 72). In Hinduism, philosophy is not just purely theoretical, it is regarded as a way of life and has practical ethical and spiritual implications. Within this context, the combination of meditation practices and philosophy is often referred to as *yoga*.

This usage of the term "yoga" is different from modern postural yoga (*asana*) as it is taught in the West today. Singleton (2010) argues that yoga *asana* evolved relatively recently out of the relationship between modern Indian nationalism and early twentieth century physical fitness movements in Europe and America.

Traditional Hindu texts refer to a variety of meditation practices. For example, the *Upanishads* mention techniques that utilise cosmic contemplation, Vedic religious symbolism, *avataras* (images understood to be a physical presence of a deity or God), and *mantras* (words or sounds that have special religious significance) such as the *OM* (Jyotirmayananda 2006). Various positive physiological and psychological effects are also mentioned in the Hindu scriptures, however health benefits tend to be the outcome of preparatory and purification practices (*kriya*) rather than of meditation itself. For example, the *Yoga Sutras* mention effects (*vibhutis*, or properties of yoga) such as the attainment of "an excellent body with grace, strength, perfect complexion and lustre" and a temperament that is "friendly and compassionate to all." However, these are seen as side effects, not primary goals of practice (Klostermaier 2007: 346–350). Body postures (*asana*) and breath control (*pranayama*) are preparatory cleansing techniques used to maintain health, prevent disease and increase the life span. However, the intention behind the cultivation of these health effects is religious; that is, the primary goal of *asana* and *pranayama* is to prepare the individual to sit comfortably and motionless for long periods of meditation. Klostermaier (2007: 140–141) notes: "That health and religion go hand in hand is a commonly accepted truism among the Hindus."

Sometimes *kriyas* contain meditative elements, such as in the case of *trataka*, which is both a purification practice and a form of concentration meditation. *Trataka* is mentioned in the *Hatha Yoga Pradipika* (c. 900–1000 B.C.E.), the first important written work to depict the *asanas* used in the Hatha Yoga tradition. It involves concentrated gazing at an object (usually a candle flame) and is said to confer a wide range of health benefits, including the treatment of eye conditions, depression, insomnia, allergies, anxiety, and postural problems.[2] When practised correctly, *trataka* also induces a meditative mental state and, with time, is said to improve memory and concentration. There is some scientific evidence to support this claim (Raghavendra and Singh 2016). However, like the other

---

[2] See Swami Muktibodhananda, *Hatha Yoga Pradipika*.

kriyas, while *trataka* has many alleged therapeutic effects, its primary purpose as a cleansing technique is connected to a religious goal; that is, to purify and prepare the body for the demands of prolonged meditation. Hence, while meditation is utilised in contemporary Western secular settings primarily for its health benefits, in the traditional Hindu context physical and mental wellbeing are required in order *to begin* meditation practice; they are not its goal.

Scholars have noted that although many discrepancies exist between traditional Hindu texts, they all point towards a common theme; that is, if an individual practises meditation with dedication, for a prolonged period of time, it should eventually lead to a state of enlightenment (*moksha,* or *mukti,* liberation). This is the primary goal of Hindu meditation.[3] Although described as a state of being that is ultimately ineffable, in Hinduism, the term "enlightenment" refers to both liberation from the cycle of rebirth (*samsara*),[4] as well as the ability to gain access to and dwell in "pure consciousness" (*purusha*; also sometimes translated as *true person* or *true self*). Sedlmeier and Srinivas (2016: 3–4) write that "gaining access to pure consciousness and dwelling therein is, in fact, the highest aim [of meditation] ... the result of having gained access to pure consciousness and dwelling therein is known in the literature as ... 'enlightenment' or 'realisation.'" Many other definitions of this state exist including "to see reality as it is," or to realise the equivalence of the small individual self (*Atman*) with one's true eternal Self (*Brahman*). According to Vedanta philosophy, all human suffering results from ignorance of, and separation from, this pure consciousness state. Pure consciousness is always present, but the conscious mind, with its constant fluctuations (*vritti*), prevents this state from being accessed. If, however, the mind is able to be stilled via meditation, then the connection between the limited human intellect and pure consciousness can become strong enough to enable the individual to access the pure consciousness state and abide there. There is a complex religious literature that details the process that leads to enlightenment, however, suffice it to say that meditation works by intercepting the flux of ordinary mental activity and allowing the mind to access states of

---

[3] However, Klostermaier (2007: 178) notes that the terms *moksa* or *mukti* are hardly ever used by the Upanishads to describe the "ultimate condition;" they prefer terms like *immortality, bliss,* or becoming *brahman.*

[4] The general Hindu and Buddhist worldview is that humans (and all sentient beings) are subject to an apparently endless cycle of rebirth or reincarnation.

meditative absorption and concentration (Sanskrit: *samadhi*) that lead to eventual liberation. Koneru Ramakrishna Rao (2010: 1142) summarises:

> Meditation in the classical tradition has a single acceptable application, which is the transformation of the person to realise herself in a state of total transcendence and freedom from all the existential constraints.

Buddhist approaches to meditation

Buddhism refers to a vast and complex religious and philosophical tradition that originated approximately 2500 years ago, and which is oriented around the teachings of the historical Buddha, Siddhartha Gautama (c.480–c.400 B.C.E.) who is believed to have lived and taught mainly in the eastern part of ancient India. Buddhism emerged out of Upanishadic traditions (what is often referred to now as "Hinduism") as a breakaway sect, and may be viewed as a form of "unorthodox Hinduism." Living Buddhism is divided into three broad traditions (*yanas*, paths/vehicles): the Theravada tradition of Southeast Asia, the Mahayana schools and the Vajrayana tradition of Tibetan Buddhism (Gethin 1998). These traditions all have various schools and sub-traditions and each approaches meditation differently. However, like the Hindu approaches, despite superficial differences, the schools of Buddhism all share a common goal: to lead the individual to a state of enlightenment (*nirvana*, or cessation of suffering). In Buddhism, this involves following a path that incorporates ethics (*sila*), the cultivation of wisdom (*prajna*) and the practice of meditation. Buddhism also contains rituals and belief in mythical cosmologies that include magic, other realms, and unseen supernatural beings who respond to prayers, invocations and offerings.

The meditation component of the Buddhist path consists of both concentration practices and insight practices, which are sometimes referred to as "right concentration" and "right mindfulness" (Sedlmeier et al. 2012). Concentration (or "calm abiding") practices (Pali: *samatha*) are generally regarded as preliminary meditations that calm and stabilise the mind. However, unlike in modern Western meditation, calmness is not cultivated as an *end in itself*, rather it is practised as preparation for insight meditation (Pali: *vipassana*). When the mind has achieved a requisite degree of stable concentration, the individual is then able to pay close enough attention to moment-to-moment mental occurrences and see into their true nature. This is the basis of *vipassana*, or "penetrating insight" practice.[5]

According to Buddhist philosophy: "One cannot know things as they really are with an unequipoised mind, for the Bhagavat [the Buddha] has proclaimed, 'The man whose mind is equipoised knows things as they really are.'" In other words, human suffering results from a distorted perception of reality. This distorted view leads the individual to live in a constant state of illusion and reproduce a never-ending cycle of rebirth (*samsara*). The path to enlightenment involves correcting these perceptual distortions and seeing reality as it really is: impermanent (*anicca*), productive of suffering (*dukkha*) and devoid of self (*anatta*). However, while Buddhist philosophy explains in detail the cause of suffering and its cure, enlightenment cannot be realised from intellectual thought alone; it must arise through direct experience of the truth of the Buddha's teachings. This requires the individual to look deeply into their own experience of reality, something that is not possible for those who have unfocused and uncultivated minds. It is only through the practice of meditation that direct insight becomes possible. In a discussion of the integration of concentration and insight meditation practices, Thurman and Gray (2006: 163–164) write:

> the mind, which is initially highly resistant to concentration meditative exercises, can initially be focused only via tremendous effort, which gradually gives rise to intermittent and finally unbroken focus of the mind on a single object. Mastery is achieved when this focus can be maintained "naturally," i.e., without any conscious effort ... From the basis of this mastery of the mind gradually achieved through quiescence exercises, one's Insight analysis is no longer purely intellectual, but is experiential, involving one's entire psychophysical complex.

Like Hinduism, Buddhism teaches that enlightenment involves freedom from human suffering and rebirth (*samsara*) as well as the recognition of an ultimate reality. However, in Buddhism, ultimate reality is experienced through the insight that all phenomena arise and pass away as a chain of conditions that ultimately can be reduced to non-existence or emptiness (*sunyata*). Although this definition seems quite

---

[5] *Bhavanakrama I* cited in Hollenback 2000: 598.

different to the Hindu concept of a pure consciousness state, as the term "enlightenment" is essentially ineffable, some scholars argue that it is possible that both traditions are speaking of the same experience; that is, that the experience of pure consciousness may be the same as that of pure emptiness. Even within the various schools of Buddhism there are disagreements regarding what enlightenment means, and what experiential states refer to true realisations of *nirvana*. For example, Burmese meditation master Mahasi Sayadaw of the Theravada Buddhist tradition maintains that *nirvana* is the cessation of all phenomena, whereas some schools of Tibetan Buddhism view enlightenment as the ability to see "all phenomena as truly beyond suffering, as an inseparable emptiness-luminosity-bliss state" (Davis and Vago 2013: 870). Similarly, Tibetan Buddhism speaks of a "primordial wisdom" (a basic state of knowing that is beyond the conceptual mind), while Zen Buddhism refers to "original mind" and "no mind." Even within Theravada Buddhism there is disagreement regarding what experiential states refer to realisations of *nirvana* and which are merely deep states of concentration (*jhana*). However, there is one common theme that exists among all the traditions. As Eleanor Rosch (2002: 32) writes: "All agree that 'this' is our original, natural, fundamental state, what we are right now, *not any particular or special experience.*"

In summary, both Hinduism and Buddhism view meditation as a practice that has short-term (state) and long-term (trait) transformational goals. The terms "state" and "trait" are modern psychological concepts deriving from scientific psychology, especially psychometric research on personality and intelligence. However, modern meditation teachers who are influenced by Western neuroscience and psychology have adopted these terms in order to differentiate between short-term and long-term changes that result from meditation (e.g. Tang et al. 2016). However, unlike in Western secular applications, changes in the short-term state (e.g. calming of the mind; *jhanas*) produced by Hindu and Buddhist meditation are cultivated as part of a much larger transformational aim: the realisation of enlightenment, or a fully transformed consciousness. Both traditions consider the everyday state of consciousness and the conventional sense of a "self" to be inaccurate, limited, and the cause of human suffering. This suffering can be overcome by following a prescribed religious path that includes many components (including ethics, ritual and renunciation), and of which meditation is a key element.

Meditation in the west: mainstream

Ideas about Eastern meditation began to infiltrate Western popular culture before the American Revolution, through various European esoteric Christian sects (Murphy and Donovan 1999). However, up until the eighteenth century, Western engagement with Eastern religions was sporadic and occurred mainly through missionaries, travel and trade (Parsons 2009). It wasn't until the nineteenth century, particularly the period between the 1840s and the 1880s, that Eastern religious philosophy and meditation practices really started to have a significant influence on Western ideas regarding spirituality and mental healing. In *Mindful America*, Jeff Wilson (2014: 15) argues that the beginnings of American interest in Buddhism are usually dated to 1844, when Edward Salisbury (1814–1901), an American Professor of Arabic and Sanskrit languages, read his *Memoir on the History of Buddhism* to the American Oriental Society, and the Transcendentalist journal *Dial* published Elizabeth Palmer Peabody's (1804–1894) translation of an extract from the Lotus Sutra. During this period popular writers and transcendentalists such as Ralph Waldo Emerson (1803–1882) and Henry David Thoreau (1817–1862) were influenced by Eastern scriptures on meditation and their works reflected a new and influential paradigm for the understanding of different religions as pointing towards a common universal metaphysical "truth" (McMahan 2008: 70–71). The idea of a perennial philosophy (*philosophia perennis*) was also promoted by the Theosophical Society, an organisation founded by Helena Blavatsky (1831–1891) and Colonel Henry Steel Olcott (1832–1907) in New York in 1875, and which greatly influenced the spread of Hindu and Buddhist ideas in the West. Blavatsky introduced Eastern concepts into American spiritualist groups and published texts on meditation, making them available in popular form to English-speaking audiences. Similarly, New Thought practitioners (followers of the American spiritual teacher Phineas P. Quimby [1802–1866]) also included meditation techniques such as guided visualisations and mantras as part of their healing therapies (Hickey 2008: 72).

The nineteenth century also saw notable visits to the West by Eastern spiritual leaders, such as Swami Vivekananda (1863–1902), the Zen *roshi* Soyen Shaku (1860–1919), and Paramahansa Yogananda (1893–1952), all of whom founded societies and institutions for the distribution of their meditation techniques and philosophical teachings. In particular, scholars have argued that the Parliament of the World's Religions, held in Chicago in 1893, was the landmark event that increased Western awareness of meditation, as this was the first time that Westerners on Western soil received Eastern spiritual teachings directly from Asian teachers. Carole Cusack (2011) argues that the event, which ran from 11–27 September, is now viewed retrospectively as the first instance of interfaith dialogue and religious pluralism. The Buddhist delegation at the Parliament was one of the more influential groups, and speakers such as Sri Lankan preacher Anagarika Dharmapala (1864–1933), Soyen Shaku and Swami Vivekananda were all very positively received. As a result, Cusack (2011: 305) notes that Buddhist sympathisers like the German American Paul Carus (1852–1919) "initiated programmes to disseminate Buddhism among Westerners, through personal relationships with both the high-profile Dharmapala, and especially Sōen."

Despite this initial interest, meditation remained a relatively fringe activity in the West until the late 1960s when there was a wave of interest in Eastern spiritual practices fuelled by the countercultural climate. Factors such as youth unrest (triggered by opposition to the Vietnam War), suspicion of organised religion, a focus on individualism and experiential knowledge, and widespread experimentation with psychedelics, combined to create a cultural climate where meditation thrived. In particular, young people who were largely brought up and educated within a Christian environment often became disillusioned with the externally imposed moral constraints and absolutist belief systems of organised religion (Oliver 2014). Instead, they began to gravitate towards psychological theory and personal experience as a way to make sense of the world. As a result, there was an increased popular interest in, and idealisation of, Eastern religions and their seemingly more liberal, diverse and experiential frameworks. Westerners were attracted to Eastern religious concepts such as non-duality and *karma*, ideals of non-violence and peace, and the focus on the individual spiritual experience. In *Hinduism and the 1960s* Paul Oliver (2014) notes that young Westerners were also attracted to stories of the mystical achievements and abilities of yogis and meditators, which were so different from normal experience in the West. Within this context, meditation began to be appreciated as both a tool for psychological growth and development, and an Eastern religious technique that could be used to directly experience the divine.

During the 1960s and 1970s the mainstreaming of meditation continued to be influenced by the arrival of Eastern religious teachers from

Asia. During this period several highly influential Eastern religious figures visited the West, including neo-Hindu guru and founder of the International Society for Krishna Consciousness (ISKCON) Srila Prabhupada (1896–1977), controversial Tibetan lama Chogyam Trungpa (1939–1987), Vietnamese monk Thich Nhat Hanh (b.1926), and Tenzin Gyatso (b.1935) the fourteenth Dalai Lama of Tibet (Cusack 2011: 307). While these spiritual teachers all played a significant role in dispersing ideas related to meditation, Maharishi Mahesh Yogi (1918–2008), the founder of Transcendental Meditation (TM), arguably had the most substantial impact on the popular reception of meditation in the West. Transcendental meditation (TM) is a form of meditation that uses a mantra to centralise cognitive focus. Scientific research studies on TM often define the technique as a concentration practice, however the TM organisation states that TM is not a concentration practice, but rather a "self-transcending" technique. The TM technique is associated exclusively with the teachings of Maharishi Mahesh Yogi, is derived from Vedantic Hinduism, and references texts such as the *Rig Veda* and Patanjali's *Yoga Sutra* (a foundational text of *yoga*, one of the six orthodox systems of Hinduism) (Williamson 2010: 95–100). Despite its Hindu roots, TM is generally described as a secular practice that is not associated with any religion or belief system. The TM website states: "The TM technique is not a religion, philosophy, or lifestyle. No belief or expectation is needed for it to be effective."[6]

Like Vivekananda and Yogananda before him, Mahesh had a Western-style education, was fluent in English, and argued that meditation was compatible with Western science. However, Mahesh's unique contribution was his ability to connect with the mainstream media, in particular the youth market. At the time, almost half of the American population was under the age of twenty-five and according to Philip Goldberg (2010: 156) "whatever captured their fancy reverberated throughout society." Hence, when Mahesh taught TM to The Beatles and other popular celebrities he obtained the "gold standard" in terms of celebrity endorsements, along with a tremendous amount of media coverage. Goldberg (2010: 161) writes that "every mention of the Beatles and meditation seemed to increase demand on campuses, where students flocked to introductory lectures, sometimes by the thousands."

---

[6] Transcendental Meditation website, https://www.tm.org/wellness-program/what-is-tm. Accessed October 2018.

The popular news media also ran numerous articles on TM, including a 1975 *TIME* magazine cover featuring an image of Mahesh along with the headline: "Meditation: The Answer to all Your Problems?" This was before the internet, a time when a story in a national magazine resulted in a huge amount of exposure. Mahesh also made appearances on national television, which resulted in an unprecedented amount of US media attention for an Eastern meditation teacher. Goldberg (2010: 158) notes:

> The mother lode was two nationally televised interviews, one with Johnny Carson on *The Tonight Show* and one with Joe Garagiola on *Today*. Likely no spiritual teacher, except perhaps the pope or Billy Graham, had ever been heard by that many Americans at once … Probably very few viewers understood what he was talking about. But the words, "more energetic," "more productive," and "happier" no doubt registered …

As a result, books about meditation and Mahesh gained mainstream popularity. The book *TM: Discovering Inner Energy and Overcoming Stress* (1975) remained on the New York Times bestseller list for six months and sold well over a million copies (Goldberg 2010: 167).

The popularity of TM could be said to have reached its peak in 1976, when more than one million people had allegedly learned to meditate using the TM method, and scientific research into meditation, and the legitimisation of meditation in general, was established. However, in the same year the cultural impact of TM began to decline. Scholars of religion argue that this happened for several reasons, including competition from the arrival of new Eastern gurus, the high cost of the introductory TM course, and a shift in the focus of the TM movement away from basic meditation and towards a new practice called the "TM-Sidhi technique" (Williamson 2010: 94–97; Wilson, 2014: 79). Further, despite the persistent framing of TM as scientific and secular, it still included quasi-religious elements such as guru-teachers, initiation ceremonies, Sanskrit mantras derived from Tantric Hinduism, a connection to ideas such as reincarnation and God-consciousness, and alleged supernatural benefits such as the ability to levitate. These factors decreased the ability of TM to penetrate into some secular areas of society and attracted criticism from both liberal and conservative Christians (Wilson 2014: 79–80).

As interest in TM declined, mainstream interest in a new type of meditation—"mindfulness" meditation—increased. Mindfulness derives from Theravada Buddhism, and is usually associated with the teachings of the Burmese monk Mahasi Sayadaw (1904–1982), the canonical text *Satipatthana Sutta* (the Discourse on the Foundations of Mindfulness), Buddhaghosa's *Visuddhimagga* (Path of Purification) and other Pali sources (Sharf 2015: 472). The *Satipatthana Sutta* is generally regarded as the canonical Buddhist text with the most comprehensive instructions on the system of mindfulness meditation. In its modern use, mindfulness is conceptualised as a type of "open monitoring" practice whereby the practitioner is attentive, moment by moment, to anything that arises in experience, without focusing on any explicit object (Lutz et al. 2008). Open monitoring involves non-reactively monitoring the contents of experience, primarily as a means to recognise emotional and cognitive patterns. While there are many disagreements regarding how to best operationally define mindfulness, a commonly accepted definition is taken from the work of Jon Kabat-Zinn (1994: 4), where mindfulness is described as "paying attention in a particular way: on purpose, in the present moment, and non-judgmentally." Kabat-Zinn's definition of mindfulness includes influences from Mahayana Buddhism, Zen, Vedanta, and select Neo-Hindu gurus (Kabat-Zinn 2011).

In *Mindful America*, Jeff Wilson (2014: 31) identifies the 1970s as the decade when mindfulness meditation first began to flourish in Western culture. He writes:

> When the decade opened, mindfulness was a marginal practice within Western Buddhism, associated with a handful of books and pamphlets, most of them by Asians or Europeans. By the end of the decade, the major players in American mindfulness were all in place, and permanent institutions dedicated to the promotion of mindfulness were beginning to make their mark. The center of the mindfulness movement was shifting toward the United States, which would soon emerge as the dominant player in the mindfulness game.

Wilson identifies several key sources of mindfulness teaching that appeared in the 1970s and which drove the contemporary Western mindfulness movement. Firstly, a number of Westerners trained in Asia in the *vipassana* meditation method, and brought the teachings home in the form of workshops and retreats for Western lay practitioners. The *vipassana* course is a standardised, residential ten-day course that is presented in a secular retreat format. It is based on Buddhist philosophy and practices derived from the Theravada Buddhist tradition. Szekeres and Wertheim (2015: 376) offer a brief description of a *vipassana* course:

> Participants meditate 10 h[ours] daily, refrain from reading and religious practices, eat vegetarian foods twice daily and remain silent during the course (except during question periods). These processes eliminate distractions that could prevent being present to moment-to-moment experiences, thereby helping to settle the mind and fostering openness to the meditative practices. During the first 3 days, students observe the natural flow of incoming and outgoing breath to develop focused attention and present-moment awareness. From day 4, students practise *Vipassana*. On day 10, loving-kindness meditation is taught.

Many Western teachers who trained in the *vipassana* method also had formal scientific training in disciplines such as psychology and medicine, as well as an extensive personal experience of meditation. Hence, this period saw the rise of a new type of Western meditation teacher; one who was trained in science but sympathetic to Eastern religions, and also personally engaged in meditation practices. In particular, the *vipassana* teachers Jack Kornfield and Joseph Goldstein have been highly influential in the mainstreaming of mindfulness. Both integrated meditative insights with Western psychology, and argued for the importance of psychological healing as part of the spiritual path. For example, Kornfield, a clinical psychologist, wrote his PhD dissertation on the phenomenology of the *vipassana* meditation experience and has argued for the need to integrate Western psychotherapeutic ideas regarding the individual psychological self into meditation practice (e.g. Kornfield 1988). In 1976, Kornfield and Goldstein (along with Sharon Salzberg and Jacqueline Schwartz) founded the Insight Meditation Society (IMS). Later, in 1981 Kornfield moved to California where he founded the Spirit Rock Meditation Center. Both IMS and Spirit Rock are highly influential organisations and have cultivated a large number of students and teachers of mindfulness meditation across America.

The second source that contributed to the mainstreaming of mindfulness meditation was the modernist Vietnamese monk Thich Nhat

Hanh, who, along with the Fourteenth Dalai Lama, became one of the most influential Buddhist teachers for non-Buddhist popular audiences. Officially exiled from Vietnam in 1973, Hanh began to teach meditation to Westerners in the mid-1970s. His teachings draw from both Mahayana and Zen Buddhism and emphasise the practice of mindfulness combined with dedicated engagement with the world—a perspective that has appealed to many modern Westerners. Wilson (2014) argues that Hanh is the most important figure in Western Buddhism in terms of direct influence, number of students taught, and impact on the language of contemporary Western Buddhism. Hanh has taught at Princeton and Colombia Universities, published more than a hundred books in English, including the 1976 book *The Miracle of Mindfulness*, and established a wide network of Buddhist practice groups known as the Community of Mindful Living.

Finally, the "universally acknowledged turning point" for the mindfulness movement's mainstreaming, and in particular its relationship with science and medicine, is 1979, when scientist Jon Kabat-Zinn founded the Stress Reduction and Relaxation Program (SR & RP). Now referred to as mindfulness-based stress reduction (MBSR), Kabat-Zinn's program was based primarily on *vipassana* courses that he had attended at IMS. The central aspect of the program is the practice of "mindfulness" meditation, defined by Kabat-Zinn (1994: 4) as "paying attention in a particular way: on purpose, in the present moment, and non-judgmentally." Mindfulness practice generally begins with observation of the breath, and then expands to include awareness of physical sensations, thoughts, and emotional states as they arise in the present moment. The shift in focus from the breath to a variety of phenomena is what distinguishes mindfulness meditation from more concentrative forms of meditation such as TM. While both mindfulness and TM involve initial concentration on a specific object (in mindfulness, the breath; in TM, a mantra), with mindfulness meditation this focus is then directed toward the entire field of awareness.

While Kabat-Zinn's initial work on mindfulness was primarily clinical, it also filtered into the mainstream. In particular, his pragmatic and "secular" definition of mindfulness has proved to be highly appealing to non-clinical popular audiences. Kabat-Zinn has authored several popular books on mindfulness including the bestselling *Full Catastrophe Living* and *Wherever You Go, There You Are*, which have sold 400,000 and 750,000 copies respectively to date. Further, scholars have argued that not only has mindfulness meditation picked up where TM left off, it has gone well beyond TM in terms of successful integration into mainstream Western society. Unlike TM, mindfulness has been effectively (and lucratively) applied "off-the-cushion" to a variety of everyday Western middle-class needs. As a result, "meditation as self-help" has become a booming commercial industry (Wilson 2014). For example, a recent report by IBISWorld estimated that in 2015, meditation-related businesses in the United States generated $984 million in revenue (Gelles 2016). Along with the traditional categories of books and CDs, there are now also meditation apps, podcasts and wearable technologies that measure brain activity during meditation practice. The large majority of these products and services have been influenced by and based on mindfulness meditation.

Mindfulness is also taught in secular settings such as the workplace and in schools. A recent study of United States workers ($n = 85,004$) found that approximately one in seven reported engagement in some form of mindfulness-based activity, such as meditation, yoga, tai chi, and qigong (Kachan et al. 2017). Other studies suggest that mindfulness-based practices may ameliorate the negative effect of stress on employees, leading to improved employee health, increased productivity, and reduced costs for employers (Klatt et al. 2015). As such, employers such as Nike and Google offer relaxation rooms for meditation practice and there has been an increase in the number of consultants offering corporate mindfulness training (Stahl 2017; Wieczner 2016). For example, the non-profit Search Inside Yourself Leadership Institute, a mindfulness training program incubated at Google, has offered two-day workshops to Fortune 500 companies, including Ford and American Express. Recent data from MeditationCapsules and Smiling Mind, two Australian organisations that provide mindfulness training to schools, demonstrates that more than 7500 teachers are using mindfulness meditation in pastoral care classes, dedicated wellbeing classes, or as a preparatory tool at the start of academic classes (Waters 2015).

The media reporting on mindfulness has been overwhelmingly positive. "Mindfulness" has become a buzzword that has produced a huge amount of interest and enthusiasm and has permeated the discourse of popular culture (Sun 2014). For example, in 2014 *TIME* magazine ran another meditation related cover, this one titled "The Mindful Revolution" along with an accompanying story detailing the extent to which mindfulness meditation has spread into the largest sectors of modern

Western society (Pickert 2014). In the same year the *Huffington Post*, a popular American news site which has its own Mindfulness news section, declared 2014 the "Year of Mindful Living" (Gregoire 2014). Hence, via mindfulness, meditation has been able to reach into nearly every institution of Western society. In 2007 a government survey reported that there were an estimated 20 million meditation practitioners in the United States and hundreds of millions worldwide (Michaelson 2014). Meditation is now almost as popular as postural yoga and is one of the world's most widely practised and researched psychological disciplines.

Meditation in the west: clinical

Scientific studies of meditation can be traced back to the 1930s, with initial research focusing on the effects of meditation on autonomic function (Paranjpe 2011). In 1935 French cardiologist Therese Brosse travelled to India to conduct studies of the physiological changes that occurred in yogis as a result of yogic and meditative practices. Brosse undertook her studies at Kaivalyadham, a yoga institute at Lonavala near Pune, India. She used a portable electrocardiogram to obtain measurements from at least one yogi—the famous Tirumalai Krishnamacharya (1888–1989) who is often referred to as the "father of modern yoga." Krishnamacharya claimed to be able to voluntarily stop his heart by using meditative techniques and Brosse's data showed support for this claim. According to her study, Krishnamacharya's heart potentials and pulse wave decreased in magnitude to approximately zero, where they stayed for several seconds before they returned to their normal magnitude. This result was believed to support the claim that the yogi was able to voluntarily control his heart to approximate cessation of contraction (Wenger et al. 1961). Similar studies were conducted in the 1950s by Gus Wenger, a physiologist from the University of California. Wenger examined four Indian yogis who also claimed to be able to voluntarily stop their heart or pulse and reported that while the subjects did not control the heart muscle directly, they were able to induce changes in certain circulatory variables by using muscular and respiratory control (Wenger et al. 1961).

In the 1950s there was also a growing interest in the potential use of meditation in psychotherapy. This was informed by an ongoing dialogue between Buddhism and psychoanalysis which centred on the work of influential Neo-Freudian psychoanalysts Karen Horney (1885–1952) and

Erich Fromm (1900–1980), both of whom were students of renowned Zen scholar Daisetz T. Suzuki (1870–1966). Influenced by their association with Suzuki, both Horney and Fromm viewed Buddhism as a culturally distinct, but comparable, form of therapy to Western psychoanalysis (Parsons 2009). This view was based on perceived similarities between the two systems of thought, most notably the idea that both Buddhism and psychoanalysis share a common aim (the alleviation of suffering and the attainment of insight) and that both use introspection as a method to achieve this goal. Within the psychoanalytic context, meditation (in particular mindfulness, *zazen* and breathing techniques) was seen as a therapeutic tool that could increase an individual's access to their unconscious mind and help to resolve psychopathology. A prevailing idea in psychoanalysis was that unconscious conflicts were the root cause of psychopathology. It was thought that meditation could "loosen" a person's defences and allow formerly repressed unconscious material to surface and be resolved. One popular view saw meditation as a free association technique that could be used to reveal the interior contents of the unconscious mind (e.g. Kutz et al. 1985; Bogart 1991).

In the 1960s and 1970s, meditation research continued to focus on both physiological and psychological effects and researchers started to conceptualise meditation in terms of current constructs in experimental psychology such as self-regulation, addiction and stress management. Notable studies from this period include those by Japanese researchers who conducted extensive electroencephalographic (EEG) studies of Zen meditators, observing changes in brain waves and testing their reactions to external stimuli. These studies suggested that *zazen*, a Buddhist form of seated meditation, induced a calm but alert state that could potentially improve social confidence, increase emotional stability and treat drug addiction (for a review of these studies see Kornfield 1977). This period also saw the birth of the humanistic and transpersonal schools of psychology. Abraham Maslow (1908–1970) and Anthony Sutich (1907–1976) founded the *Journal of Humanistic Psychology* in 1961 and the American Association of Humanistic Psychology in 1963, in an attempt to establish a "Third Force" in American psychology; that is, an approach that focused on future-oriented self-actualisation rather than past-oriented psychopathology (Kripal 2007: 137–151). Transpersonal psychology provided a "Fourth Force" that focused on the transpersonal and spiritual dimensions of human existence. The transpersonal movement emerged out of the encounter between Western psychology,

Eastern contemplative traditions, and the psychedelic counterculture of California in the 1960s. Both humanistic and transpersonal psychology acknowledged the importance of spirituality and utilised meditative techniques such as self-awareness and mindfulness in their practices.

The 1970s also saw a significant upsurge in research on TM, with studies indicating that this form of meditation could decrease blood pressure, respiratory rate, and anxiety, while increasing self-actualisation and other positive behavioural outcomes in a large variety of domains. (For a review of some of these studies see Shapiro and Walsh 2009). In particular, TM was to establish an enduring presence in Western medicine and psychology during this period via the work of cardiologist and academic Herbert Benson, who coined the term "relaxation response" to describe the physiological and psychological effects that occur during TM. Benson's work greatly influenced the modern Western conceptualisation of meditation as a scientifically endorsed stress reduction technique. As Goldberg (2010: 164) notes:

> [TM] was presented as a scientific procedure, with results as predictable as those of any medicine, and no bad side effects. This rebranding of meditation was the first step in the secularisation and medicalisation of yogic disciplines.

Goldberg argues that the relaxation message impressed both the general public and the scientific community, and quickly overshadowed any more "profound" or spiritual reasons for meditating. Hence, by 1976 the TM movement had enough data to be able to publish a seven hundred page volume of research papers from fifty-one institutions in thirteen countries, reinforcing meditation's new role as a health and wellness intervention.

The late 1970s was also a critical period for the scientific study of mindfulness meditation. As discussed above, mindfulness was first incorporated into medical care in the form of what is now known as MBSR, an eight-week program developed by Jon Kabat-Zinn in 1979. Initially designed to treat chronic pain, the program produced promising results and over the next three decades mindfulness replaced TM as the most researched form of meditation. More recently, the success of MBSR has stimulated the development of other mindfulness-inspired clinical interventions including mindfulness-based cognitive therapy (MBCT), acceptance and commitment therapy (ACT), dialectical behaviour therapy (DBT), mindfulness-based relapse prevention (MBRP), mindfulness-based eating awareness training (MB-Eat), and mindfulness-based therapeutic community treatment. These therapies have shown efficacy in the treatment of a number of conditions including depression, anxiety, chronic pain, substance abuse, eating disorders, addiction and psychosis. Today, MBSR is an established practice in hospitals and a large number of clinicians have undertaken training in mindfulness-based interventions. In the United Kingdom mindfulness has also been adopted by the NHS, with many primary care trusts offering and recommending the practice instead of cognitive behavioural therapy. Additionally, mindfulness meditation research has expanded from looking at how mindfulness can improve outcomes for a variety of illnesses, to looking at how mindfulness might improve performance enhancement in healthy populations.

While the majority of meditation research is still on mindfulness, the field has also expanded to include the study of other Buddhist-derived meditation techniques, such as practices aimed at the cultivation of compassion (for example, *metta*, or loving-kindness meditation: e.g. Kabat-Zinn 2017), and other analytical styles of meditation (for example, deity visualisation practices: e.g. Kozhevnikov et al. 2009). New areas of research such as technological approaches to mindfulness training are emerging, and discussions are taking place regarding the field of "contemplative science" and how to best define, classify, and study a variety of meditation practices (Dorjee 2016). Recently there has been an increased interest in the study of contemplative practices within neuroscience, psychology, and the health sciences, which has resulted in the development of several new academic journals including *Mindfulness, The Journal of Compassionate Healthcare,* and the *Journal of Contemplative Inquiry* (Ozawa-de Silva 2016).

CHAPTER TWO

The dark side of dharma: meditation adverse effects and the "dark night"

> *The Dark Night can really fuck up your life.*
> —Daniel M. Ingram.[7]

The meditation backlash

While the general attitude towards secular meditation has been overwhelmingly positive, there has been some criticism. In particular, critics have raised concerns regarding whether meditation can ever be truly secular (Hale 2018), the integrity and effectiveness of so-called secular approaches (Hyland 2017; Wilks 2014), and whether Buddhists and Hindus might be covertly imposing their religious views under the guise of healthcare or psychology. For example, some Hindu purists have accused the founder of TM, Maharishi Mahesh Yogi, of watering down the Hindu tradition and of "selling mantras" (Goldberg 2010: 160). Other scholars are concerned that mindfulness has been diluted and commodified to such an extent that it places the blame for all suffering onto the individual and distracts from the worldly, societal causes of

---

[7] Ingram, D.M. *Mastering the Core Teachings of the Buddha: An Unusually Hardcore Dharma Book.* London, UK: Aeon Books Ltd, 2018: 215.

stress and anxiety (Purser 2019). Additionally, the scientific research on meditation has not been universally accepted, with critics pointing to a variety of methodological flaws, including inadequate control groups, small sample sizes, demographic homogeneity among participants, inattention to gender as a variable, and researcher bias. These criticisms apply to all meditation studies, including those that have found adverse effects. For example, Goyal et al. (2014) conducted a systematic review and meta-analysis of forty-seven mindfulness studies and found no evidence that meditation programs were better than any active treatment such as medication, exercise, and other behavioural therapies. Finally, there is the criticism that is the focus of this book. That is, some meditation teachers and researchers have begun to discuss potential adverse effects associated with secular meditation practices, including profound but de-stabilising insights, problematic spiritual emergencies, and the exacerbation of pre-existing mental health issues. In their recent book *Meditation, Buddhism and Science,* David McMahan and Erik Braun (2017: 13) write: "A note of caution has emerged regarding recommending extensive meditation for all, no matter what one's psychological condition."

Negative effects related to meditation have been described across a variety of religious traditions and in modern Western psychology. Terms such as "Dark Night of the Soul," "Kundalini Crisis," and "Spiritual Emergency" have all been used to refer to periods of difficulty associated with contemplative practice. In contemporary Western meditation-based convert Buddhist lineages[8] the term "dark night" has recently been adopted in order to describe a variety of meditation-related difficulties. While the term dark night is not a Buddhist term—rather it is an abbreviated form of the expression "dark night of the soul" and derives from Christian mysticism—it has recently been appropriated in popular postmodern Buddhist discourses. The Buddhist dark night is referred to in a range of media including popular news articles, discussion forums, blogs, podcasts, books, and meditation manuals written by well-known contemporary meditation teachers. Despite the proliferation of the phrase, there has been much confusion regarding what

---

[8] The term "Western meditation-based convert Buddhist lineages" is used by Ann Gleig (2019: 7) to describe "convert" or "white" Buddhism as practiced predominantly by Euro-Americans. Gleig writes that "Converts are concerned with seeking enlightenment and focus heavily on meditation practice."

the term dark night actually refers to in a postmodern Buddhist context.[9] During the course of my research I attempted to "delineate the Buddhist dark night" and found that there are currently three dominant discourses regarding the dark night in Buddhist postmodernism: 1) the *"dukkha nana"* discourse; 2) the "insight gone wrong" discourse; and 3) the meditation "adverse effects" discourse. While these discourses appear on the surface to be quite different, they are linked by a common theme; that is, an attempt to differentiate between Buddhist meditation-related difficulties and Western psychopathology.

The dark night of the soul

The expression "dark night of the soul" derives from Christian mysticism and commonly refers to a poem and theological commentary written by the 16th-century Spanish mystic and poet St. John of the Cross (1542–1591). The poem—*La Noche Oscura del Alma*—describes the difficult journey of the soul in its quest to reach mystical union with God. This is a journey that involves periods of profound spiritual suffering and desolation. While there are various analyses of St John's dark night, in general it is interpreted as referring to a profound feeling of spiritual dryness or the absence of God (e.g. Coe 2000). This feeling of alienation and despair has been described as the "darkness of midnight when detachment has left us all alone and all is lost" (Dombrowski 1992: 30). At its most extreme the dark night may become a crisis of faith and result in intense doubt regarding the spiritual path. Historically, many saints and seekers—for example, Mother Theresa and St Teresa of Avila—have spoken of such experiences of spiritual darkness. In the Christian tradition, these dark periods are recognised as periods of great spiritual development.

---

[9] While scholars such as David McMahan have referred to "Buddhist Modernism" (a form of Buddhism that has resulted from the encounter between traditional Buddhism and Western modernity under colonialism) Gleig (2019) argues that there are clear indications that convert Buddhist lineages have passed the modern age and are now postmodern. Themes that are more suggestive of postmodernism (for example, globalism, the adoption of technology, recognition of diversity, and a renewed interest in tradition) are certainly found in the Buddhist "dark night" discourses. Hence while there is much debate regarding the relationship of postmodernity to modernity I choose to adopt the term "Buddhist Postmodernism" when referring to the neo-Buddhist practices, figures and communities described in this chapter.

In the 1960s and 1970s the term "dark night of the soul" transcended the Christian spiritual tradition from which it originated and was integrated into modern Western psychology. Specifically the term was adopted by transpersonal psychologists interested in "spiritual crisis" or "spiritual emergence." Stanislav and Christina Grof (1989) coined the term "spiritual emergence" in order to describe a period of significant distress associated with a spiritual awakening. According to Grof and Grof, spiritual crisis or emergence occurs when an individual's process of spiritual growth and change becomes chaotic and overwhelming, resulting in disruption to psychological, social, and occupational functioning. While the manifestations of spiritual crisis are highly individual and no two spiritual crises are exactly the same, there are some common features that appear for most people. These include a loss of sense of identity, radically changing personal values, and the occurrence of mystical and spiritual experiences. Mentions of the dark night of the soul can be found in the transpersonal spiritual crisis literature and these mentions usually refer to St John of the Cross' dark night as a classic example of a spiritual crisis.

In the transpersonal psychology paradigm, a dark night may occur for any individual who is on a spiritual path and, as a result, is engaged in a personal spiritual transformative process. This process may include unusual and distressing states of consciousness that traditional Western psychiatry would normally define as psychopathology. However, Grof and Grof (1989: x) argue that such experiences are actually crises of personal transformation: "Episodes of this kind have been described in sacred literature of all ages as a result of meditative practices and as signposts of the mystical path." Italian psychiatrist and transpersonal pioneer Roberto Assagioli (1989: 39–40) refers to the dark night as a stage of growth, a purification process, and a "divine homesickness." Transpersonal psychologist Ken Wilber (1993: 149) describes to the dark night as an "abandonment depression" that occurs when one's experience of the divine begins to fade. It is important to note that while transpersonal psychology references the divine, the transpersonal dark night is less concerned with traditional notions of God and organised religion and more with a transformation of the private psychological self. The transpersonal dark night may involve a loss of spiritual or religious faith, but it also refers more generally to a loss in one's sense of personal identity, life direction, and purpose. Hence, the transpersonal dark night contains spiritual elements, but it's a private, mystical, individualised spirituality that has emerged from the sociological interaction between Eastern/shamanic traditions and a Western psychological worldview.

The dukkha nanas

The dark night first made its appearance in postmodern Buddhism with the work of American Buddhist teacher Jack Kornfield. Kornfield is a teacher in the American *vipassana* movement, a former Theravada monk, and founding member of the Insight Meditation Society. Part of the baby boomer generation of American dharma teachers, Kornfield has been at the forefront of a movement that attempts to integrate the traditional teachings of Buddhism with the secular humanistic values of Western psychology. Gleig (2013) argues that Kornfield's approach has re-visioned the Buddhist goal of enlightenment from a transcendental condition that demands world renunciation, to an embodied enlightenment that is possible for lay practitioners in everyday life. As such, Kornfield's focus is on the integration of spiritual insight into worldly life and the challenges that may accompany this integration.

Kornfield brought the term dark night into popular postmodern Buddhist vernacular in 1989 when he wrote a chapter for Grof and Grof's (1989) classic text *Spiritual Emergency: When Personal Transformation Becomes a Crisis*. Titled "Obstacles and Vicissitudes in Spiritual Practice," Kornfield's chapter details a variety of difficulties on the spiritual path and briefly mentions the term dark night in relation to the Theravada *dukkha nanas* (Pali: insights into suffering), a series of insights that are characterised by fear, misery and disgust and which can cause mental distress. As a meditator progresses through the *dukkha nanas*, they can expect to experience a range of challenging perceptual, emotional and psychological changes. The *dukkha nanas* are well-documented in Buddhist manuals such as the *Visuddhimagga* (The Path of Purification), the *Vimuttimaga* (The Path of Freedom), and the *Abidhamma*, and are usually interpreted as milestones on the path to enlightenment. In his (1993a) book *A Path With Heart* Kornfield is more explicit about the connection between the dark night and the *dukkha nanas*. In this text he refers to the dark night as part of a process of death and rebirth which occurs during insight meditation and which involves the gradual dissolution of personal identity. This painful process involves cycling through the *dukkha nanas*.

In *After the Ecstasy, the Laundry*, a book which focuses on life after spiritual awakening, Kornfield (2000) uses the term dark night to refer to a more general sense of darkness and loss that occurs with the fading of mystical experiences. As scholars and mystics will attest, all mystical peak experiences are inevitably followed by a return to a conventional state of consciousness and to "normal" life. Memories of ecstatic mystical states tend to fade with time, and the individual is left with the mundane task of integrating spiritual insights into everyday life. Similar to Assagioli's "divine homesickness" and Wilber's "abandonment depression," here Kornfield (2000: 113) uses the term dark night to refer to the "long painful periods in which we lose our sense of connection with the Divine." However, there is still a connection to the *dukkha nanas* as Kornfield draws attention to the cyclical nature of the contemplative path. He notes that the progress of insight is not linear but "circular and continuous" and as one progresses one will face a fluctuating series of exalted mystical states and future dark nights (Kornfield 2000: 116).

The use of the term dark night to describe the *dukkha nanas* has been developed further by Daniel Ingram, an experienced meditator in the *vipassana* tradition and a founder of the "Pragmatic Dharma" movement: a movement that emphasises a secular, practical, and transparent approach to meditation practice. While he does not identify as a dharma teacher, Ingram is the author of a popular meditation manual *Mastering the Core Teachings of the Buddha (MCTB)* and the founder of the Dharma Overground,[10] a website which includes a forum where meditation practitioners can discuss their experiences. Ingram's personal style is reflective of the characteristics of Gen X dharma teachers, who, compared to the baby boomer generation are "much less performative as teachers and much more comfortable with personal disclosure" (Gleig 2019: 222). Hence, *MCTB* provides an exceptionally detailed description of the *dukkha nanas*, and the perceptual, emotional and cognitive challenges that accompany these stages of insight. In the Gen X spirit of full dharma disclosure, Ingram also discusses his own personal experiences with the dark night in *MCTB* ("I was a chronic Dark Nighter for over ten years") and on the Dharma Overground forums (Ingram 2018: 234). At the time of writing, the Dharma Overground category "Dealing with the Dark Night" had 218 individual threads dedicated to the topic of the dark night.[11]

---

[10] *Dharma Overground* at https://www.dharmaoverground.org/. Accessed July 2019.
[11] *Dharma Overground* at https://www.dharmaoverground.org/discussion/-/message_boards/category/89581. Accessed July 2019.

Like Kornfield, Ingram takes the view that the dark night is not just a phenomenon that happens on the meditation cushion; if unresolved it can "bleed through" and impact the everyday personal life of a meditation practitioner, causing long-lasting emotional disturbances. Further, for some people the effects of the *dukkha nanas* may get intermeshed with pre-existing psychological issues, leading to a state that can be "so overwhelming as to preclude normal functioning" (Ingram 2018: 215). Ingram writes that effects of the *dukkha nanas* may "haunt" practitioners in their daily life, "sapping their energy and motivation, and perhaps even causing feelings of unease, depression, paranoia, and even suicidal thoughts" (Ingram 2018: 221). In extreme cases this may result in a practitioner making "radical life changes that cannot be easily undone, such as a divorce or firing off angry emails to your boss" (Ingram 2018: 230).

Both Kornfield and Ingram refer to dark night "cycles," and in *MCTB* Ingram describes these cycles in great detail. He notes a major problem that can occur with the dark night; that is, a meditator may get stuck in a dark night cycle—a situation which prevents the progress of insight and leads to the meditator becoming a "Dark Night yogi" or a "darknighter" (Ingram 2018: 212). Until the meditator figures out how to transition through this stage successfully by reaching the first stage of enlightenment (stream entry) they will cycle repeatedly through this dark night phase. Ingram argues that this progression appears to be a "hardwired part of human physiology" and "if meditators stop practicing entirely at this stage, they can get stuck and haunted for the rest of their lives until they complete this first progress of insight" (Ingram 2018: 233). A meditator who gets stuck in the dark night for a long time is referred to as a "chronic Dark Nighter" (Ingram 2018: 233–234). Similarly, in *A Path With Heart* Kornfield (1993a: 150–151) argues that it is important to have a knowledgeable meditation teacher and guide, otherwise it is possible to get overwhelmed by the *dukkha nanas* and quit meditation practice altogether. He warns that if an individual quits meditation during this stage:

> they [the *dukkha nanas*] will continue to haunt us. They can easily become entangled with our personal loss and fear in our everyday life. In this way, they can become undercurrents in our consciousness, and the unresolved feelings can last for months or years, until we do something to take ourselves back to this process and complete it.

This idea of the dark night becoming entangled with various aspects of one's life is a theme that is explored in more detail by Ingram, who writes about "off the cushion" meditation effects and their interaction with both psychopathology and general non-pathological psychological content. In *MCTB* Ingram attempts to differentiate between dark night symptoms (meditation-related) and personal issues and circumstances (not meditation-related). He argues that if an individual continues to practise meditation, true dark night symptoms should resolve themselves rather quickly, hence in this sense they can be differentiated from psychopathology:

> Occasionally, people at this stage can also have what appears to be a full psychotic break, or what is often called a nervous breakdown, though if these are truly a side effect of insight practices, they should pass quickly (Ingram 2018: 231).

According to transpersonal psychologists, a hallmark of a spiritual crisis is that it does eventually resolve and lead to positive transformation. Hence, in this way it can be differentiated from psychopathology, which may be lifelong and only responsive to medical intervention. Ingram (2018: 234) also notes that not all psychological distress can be attributed to the dark night:

> On the other hand, genuine mental illness or unrelated emotional or psychological difficulties can show up in people's lives. Blaming it all on the Dark Night may not always be accurate or helpful.

Ingram suggests that in some cases meditators may be better served by seeking qualified medical and psychological support, or medication.

Insight gone wrong

American meditation teacher Shinzen Young provides a different definition of the Buddhist dark night. According to his website, Young is "a Jewish-American Buddhist teacher who got turned on to comparative mysticism by an Irish-Catholic priest and who has developed a Burmese-Japanese fusion practice inspired by the spirit of quantified science."[12] Young's teachings are meditation-focused and centred on the practice of mindfulness meditation.

---

[12] Shinzen Young at https://www.shinzen.org/about/. Accessed July 2019.

Contrary to Kornfield and Ingram, Young (2011) does not consider ordinary experiences with the *dukkha nanas* or the cycles of insight to be significant enough to be referred to as a dark night. He writes:

> It is certainly the case that almost everyone who gets anywhere with meditation will pass through periods of negative emotion, confusion, disorientation, and heightened sensitivity to internal and external arisings. It is also not uncommon that at some point, within some domain of experience, for some duration of time, things may get worse before they get better. The same thing can happen in psychotherapy and other growth modalities. For the great majority of people, the nature, intensity, and duration of these kinds of challenges is quite manageable. I would not refer to these types of experiences as "Dark Night."[13]

Rather, Young reserves the term dark night for a phenomenon that he describes as more serious, potentially disabling, and considerably rarer; that is, the misinterpretation of the Buddhist insights of emptiness (*sunyata*) and non-self (*annica*). In Buddhism, gaining insight into the nature of emptiness and non-self is a positive thing and should be experienced as liberating. However, Young (2011) argues that occasionally these insights can be misunderstood by meditation practitioners, leading to a state that is sometimes referred to as "falling into the pit of the void." This state entails:

> an authentic and irreversible insight into Emptiness and No Self. What makes it problematic is that the person interprets it as a bad trip. Instead of being empowering and fulfilling, the way Buddhist literature claims it will be, it turns into the opposite. In a sense, it's Enlightenment's Evil Twin. This is serious but still manageable through intensive, perhaps daily, guidance under a competent teacher. In some cases it takes months or even years to fully metabolize, but in my experience the results are almost always highly positive.

Here Young also draws a parallel with the clinical condition depersonalisation and derealisation disorder (DP/DR). In his popular YouTube

---

[13] Shinzen Young, "The Dark Night," 13/11/2011, at https://www.shinzen.org/the-dark-night/. Accessed December 2019.

video titled "Enlightenment, DP/DR & Falling Into the Pit of the Void" he refers to DP/DR as "enlightenment's evil twin."[14] In psychiatry, DP/DR is a mental illness and is defined by the *Diagnostic and Statistical Manual of Mental Disorders, Fifth Edition* (DSM-V) as a dissociative disorder. Its essential features are "persistent or reoccurring episodes of depersonalisation, derealisation, or both" (DSM-V 2013: 302). Episodes of depersonalisation are characterised by a feeling of unreality or detachment from one's self, whereas episodes of derealisation are characterised by a feeling of unreality or detachment from the world. Young proposes that both Buddhist enlightenment and DP/DR might result from the same realisation or insight, however, the lived experience of DP/DR is the diametric opposite of the lived experience of enlightenment. While enlightenment is experienced as liberating, DP/DR is experienced as pathological. While Young does not offer an explanation for why enlightenment might "go wrong" in this way, other studies suggest that the meaning attributed to a meditation experience might affect its interpretation and subsequent affective valence (e.g. Castillo 1990).

Young (2009) posits that descriptions that match the "pit of the void" condition, or DP/DR, are found in classical Buddhist literature, including the Pali Canon, although he does not provide any further detail on where such descriptions might be found. However, similar problems associated with the insight into emptiness can be found in Buddhist literature and have been noted by Buddhist scholars. For example, Robert Sharf (2015: 470–484) mentions a similar state—"falling into emptiness" (*duokong*)—which is described in the medieval Hongzhou school of Zen. *Duokong* is said to arise from unbalanced meditation practice; specifically, it occurs when a meditator places excessive focus on achieving "inner stillness" (*ningji*) at the expense of engagement with the scriptures (Sharf 2015: 476). Further, *duokong* is associated with "meditation sickness," a term that has been used by various Buddhist masters to critique practices that they considered detrimental to contemplative progress. Sharf (2015: 476–477) writes:

> Today we might translate "meditation sickness" as "zoning out," by which I do not mean being lost in thought or daydreaming. Rather,

---

[14] Shinzen Young, "Enlightenment, DP/DR & Falling Into the Pit of the Void," 3/12/2009, at https://www.youtube.com/watch?v=9zIKQCwDXsA. Accessed December 2019. At the time of writing, this video had 45,026 views.

I suspect that when medieval meditation masters used terms such as "falling into emptiness" and "meditation sickness," they were targeting techniques that resulted in an intense immersion in the moment, in the now, such that the practitioner loses touch with the socially, culturally, and historically constructed world in which he or she lives. The practitioner becomes estranged from the web of social relations that are the touchstone of our humanity as well as our sanity. The key to avoiding this is to learn to see both sides at once. Zongmi says: "While awakening from delusion is sudden, the transformation of an unenlightened person into an enlightened person is gradual."

The Buddhist saint Nargajuna (c. 150–250 CE), one of the most important and influential Mahayana philosophers, also spoke of the potential problems associated with emptiness. Nargajuna is credited with saying that "emptiness misunderstood destroys the slow-witted, like a serpent wrongly held or a spell wrongly executed" (Siderits and Katsura 2013: 274). That is, the failure to correctly grasp the insight into emptiness (which, like a serpent, is notoriously slippery) may have dangerous consequences. For example, contemporary Buddhist meditation teacher Lewis Richmond argues that emptiness may be misinterpreted as a nihilism regarding all phenomena which may then lead to feelings of depression, anxiety, and dissociation. In an article for *Buddha Weekly*, he writes:

> If we can't understand such a profound concept, we often "lazily" associate Emptiness with Nihilism. The problem begins with the English translation of the original Sanskrit term Shunyata. This profound and complex concept is often translated into English as "voidness." Voidness sounds a lot like "nothingness" and, in my many years of attending teachings, I've often heard teachers interchange the word Emptiness, Voidness and Nothingness, so this can be confusing from the get-go. In the same discussion, some teachers will warn against nihilism, but never-the-less use the word "nothingness." There is really no adequate word in English for Shunyata, as both "voidness" and "emptiness" have negative connotations, whereas, shunyata is a positive sort of emptiness transcending the duality of positive-negative.

While Young's definition of the dark night refers to a relatively rare and quite extreme phenomenon, a more common and less intense form of "insight gone wrong" may be a lingering nihilistic attitude which arises from misunderstanding emptiness to mean that nothing in the world has a real existence. According to meditation teachers, becoming stuck in either of these dark nights can destroy a meditator's chances of progress and liberation. Hence, "as novice snake-handlers and apprentice sorcerers can attest, serpents and magic spells are dangerous instruments in the hands of those who lack the requisite knowledge" (Siderits and Katsura 2013: 274).

"Adverse effects" in meditation research

The term dark night has also been appropriated in Buddhist postmodernism as an umbrella term that encompasses a wide variety of meditation-related adverse effects. Historically, research into meditation has tended to emphasise beneficial outcomes rather than the processes involved or potential adverse effects. However, there is a growing body of evidence that suggests there may be side effects associated with meditation practice, in both clinical and non-clinical settings. The use of the term "adverse effects" in Western meditation research can be traced back to Leon Otis who used the term in his 1984 study of TM meditators, and Deane Shapiro who referred to adverse effects in his 1992 study of *vipassana* meditators. More recently, Lindahl and colleagues (2017: 1) have described meditation adverse effects as meditation experiences that are "challenging, difficult, distressing, functionally impairing, and/or requiring additional support." In their recent study *The Varieties of Contemplative Experience*, Lindahl et al. (2017: 3–4) note:

> Meditation-related effects that are not health-related benefits or that are reported as distressing have been classified as "side effects" or "adverse effects" (AEs), especially in clinical psychology research.

In this particular study the authors describe fifty-nine meditation-related experiences across seven domains: cognitive, perceptual, affective, somatic, conative, sense of self, and social. These experiences range from very positive to very negative. Following Lindahl et al. (2017), throughout this book I have chosen to adopt the term "adverse effects" for its utility, as it encompasses the widest possible spectrum of negative outcomes that may occur with meditation. Further, it is a relatively value-neutral term (as opposed to "Dark Night of the Soul" or

"Spiritual Emergence") and is not tied to any specific religious tradition (like "Kundalini Crisis").

Close examination of the scientific literature reveals that even in early meditation research, adverse effects were identified in therapeutic contexts. Notably, renowned psychologists Arnold Lazarus (1932–2013) and Albert Ellis (1913–2007), co-founders of Cognitive Behaviour Therapy (CBT), both expressed concerns regarding negative side effects associated with therapeutic meditation. For example, in 1976 Lazarus reported that some of his patients had severe disturbances after practising TM, including depression and suicidal ideation, leading in one case to a serious suicide attempt. He wrote:

> [meditation] is not a panacea. In fact, when used indiscriminately, there are clinical indications that the procedure can precipitate serious psychiatric problems such as depression, agitation, and even schizophrenic decompensation (Lazarus 1976: 601–602).

Lazarus was also one of the first researchers to argue that individual differences should be taken into account when deciding whether meditation is an appropriate intervention, noting:

> Scientific psychology has emphasized the significance of *individual differences*. Folklore is equally aware that "one man's meat is another man's poison." Yet popular systems and movements from psychoanalysis to Transcendental Meditation (TM) generalize and universalize, present their views and findings in absolutistic rather than probabilistic terms, and depart from established scientific pathways in several other respects. Their procrustean deftness at fitting everyone to their system damages the integrity and individuality of persons who are temperamentally and otherwise unsuited to their procedures (Lazarus 1976: 601).

In 1984, Ellis also expressed concerns regarding the therapeutic use of meditation, arguing that it had the potential to be more harmful than many other psychological techniques because of its association with spirituality and religion. Specifically, he argued that the traditional spiritual goals associated with meditation (such as transcendence or the experience of a higher consciousness) were probably "illusory" and "highly disturbed" since no human was likely to achieve them

(2009 [1984]: 692). Hence, he concluded that meditation combined with mysticism "includes highly dangerous, anti-therapeutic elements" (2009 [1984]: 672). However, Ellis was broadly supportive of the use of secular meditation in therapy, but like Lazarus, argued that the practice could be harmful for certain groups of individuals, particularly those with obsessive-compulsive and ruminative tendencies, noting: "A few of my own clients have gone into dissociative semi-trance states and upset themselves considerably by meditating" (2009 [1984]: 672). Interestingly, Ellis argued that the greatest potential danger of meditation was that it was "a highly palliative procedure;" that is, a diversionary technique that helped people to feel better temporarily, but that ultimately distracted them from developing the necessary skills required to make significant positive change in their lives (2009 [1984]: 672).

A more severe example of the potential adverse effects of meditation was reported in a 1975 case study by Alfred French and colleagues. The authors describe the case of a thirty-nine year old woman who, several weeks after starting TM practice, experienced altered reality testing and behaviour. While the patient had no pre-existing clinical issues, after starting meditation she experienced euphoric fantasies with mystical elements, dysphoric moods, and unusual behaviour that resembled psychosis. The authors argue that the continued presence of an altered state of consciousness, which began within days of starting TM, and the occurrence of "waking fantasies" which began shortly after, suggest a causal relationship between meditation and the subsequent psychosis-like experience, cautioning that "this form of meditation carries the risk of psychosis-like and potentially dangerous regression" (French et al. 1975: 55–58). However, the authors also emphasise that the psychosis-like symptoms appeared to be the result of a specific meditation-induced phenomenon and were distinct from standard clinical definitions of psychosis, writing: "such 'trips,' while often clinically psychosis-like, are distinct clinical entities from functional psychoses" (French et al. 1975: 55–58).

Another study of TM by Leon Otis (1984) reported that adverse effects such as pervasive anxiety and depression occurred in a significant percentage of people who practiced TM (slightly less than half of the 1,900 subjects), and that the probability of such effects occurring was higher among psychiatric populations. Of particular interest is Otis's finding that more adverse effects occurred among long-term meditators and TM teacher trainees than among novice meditators. He writes:

> These data suggest that the longer a person stays in TM and the more committed a person becomes to TM as a way of life (as indicated by the teacher trainee group), the greater the likelihood that he or she will experience adverse effects. This contrasts sharply with the promotional statements promulgated widely by the SIMS (Students International Meditation Society), IMS (International Meditation Society), WPEC (World Plan Executive Council), and related TM organisations that TM is a simple, innocuous procedure (Otis 2009 [1984]: 204).

Additionally, he noted that some participants in his study continued to practice meditation despite experiencing adverse effects, and had "compared meditation to a drug addiction ... not wishing to continue but unable to stop" (Otis 2009 [1984]: 207).

Dissociative symptoms have also been reported as a result of meditation practice. Arthur Deikman (1963) reported cases in which depersonalisation and derealisation occurred in individuals practising an experimental procedure based on classical descriptions of contemplative meditation. Raymond Kennedy (1976) also reported two meditation-related cases in which patients experienced depersonalisation and derealisation, including out-of-body experiences, and required psychiatric treatment. Additionally, Richard Castillo (1990) conducted interviews with six TM meditators and concluded that meditation can cause both depersonalisation and derealisation, and that the depersonalised state can become an apparently permanent mode of functioning. Interestingly, he noted that this permanent mode of depersonalisation can occur without there being any significant anxiety or impairment in social or occupational functioning—the meaning that the meditator attributes to the experience will determine to a great extent whether anxiety or distress is part of the experience.

Adverse effects have also been found among meditation retreat participants. For example, Deane Shapiro (1992) conducted a study on a non-clinical population ($n = 27$) at a *vipassana* meditation retreat and found that 62.9% of participants experienced at least one adverse psychological effect from meditation, including feelings of anxiety, panic, depression, confusion, and disorientation. Two participants (7% of the sample studied) experienced symptoms so severe that they stopped meditating; one participant said the retreat left him "totally disoriented ... confused, spaced out," while the other participant reported "lots of depression, confusion ... severe shaking and energy releasing" (Shapiro 1992: 64). Shapiro also found a trend that, while not statistically significant, lent support to Otis's earlier finding that meditators who had practised the longest (in this case, over 8.5 years) reported the highest frequency of adverse effects.

More recently, Tim Lomas and colleagues (2015) conducted a study on the effects of meditation (including mindfulness techniques) in a non-clinical population ($n = 30$) and found that while meditation was portrayed overall as a beneficial activity, all participants found it challenging at least some of the time. Additionally, one quarter of participants in the study encountered "substantial difficulties" with meditation, including troubling experiences of self, troubling thoughts and feelings which were hard to manage, the exacerbation of mental health issues such as depression and anxiety, and in two cases, psychosis requiring hospitalisation (Lomas et al. 2015).

Several recent studies have also looked at the re-experiencing of trauma as a potential adverse effect of meditation. Specifically, there has been recognition that meditation might cause emotional flooding (Britton and Sydnor 2015) or re-traumatisation (Treleaven 2010) in certain individuals. Jane Compson (2014) argues that in particular, intensive, silent meditation retreats may leave meditators at risk for traumatic activation, which manifests as panic, anxiety, rage, and insomnia. In his book *Trauma-Sensitive Mindfulness*, David Treleaven (2018) argues that mindfulness meditation, practised without an awareness of trauma, can exacerbate symptoms of traumatic stress, leading to flashbacks, dissociation and re-traumatisation. Treleaven (2010) also describes a specific meditation-induced phenomenon he terms "contemplative dissociation," which he defines as "a disconnection between thoughts, emotions and physical sensations that is exacerbated by contemplative practice."

In a comprehensive review of meditation adverse effects, M. Kathleen Lustyk and colleagues (2009) consulted seventeen primary publications and five secondary reports and literature reviews, including several of the studies mentioned above. The authors found that the most frequently reported meditation adverse effects were mental health issues, with the more serious cases including severe affective and anxiety disorders (for example, mania and PTSD), temporary dissociative states, and psychosis. They also reported meditation-related adverse effects on physical health, including increased epileptogenesis (risk of seizures), somatic discomfort arising from holding a meditation postural position, and potential problems associated with loss of appetite, reduced food intake, and difficulty sleeping. The authors referenced studies in which adverse spiritual health effects were reported, most notably cases of religious delusions, however they also noted that some people may fear violating their own religious principles by engaging in secular meditation practices that were originally derived from Buddhism or other religions.

It is unclear whether the effects of meditation practices alone can be compared directly with meditation practices in the context of mindfulness-based interventions (MBIs). There are very few reports of adverse effects in MBIs, though some studies do exist. For example, Leigh Burrows (2017) conducted a study examining the mindfulness meditation experiences of community college students ($n = 13$) and found that the majority of students reported negative experiences including increased heart rate, depersonalisation, disorientation, disconnection, self-other boundary dissolution, a loss of spontaneity, a loss of sense of self, and emotional flooding. Additionally, in a 2016 article Burrows noted:

> Results from this small qualitative study showed 12 of the 13 participants who chose to participate reported a range of unusual perceptions, sensations, and altered states and experiences of self as a result of mindfulness meditation. Only one participant reported unambiguously positive effects such as increased relaxation, focused attention, productivity, and reduction in stress and worry.

Other recent studies of mindfulness meditation have reported increases in perceived stress and depression and feelings of exhaustion or disorientation (Dobkin et al. 2012), increased false memory susceptibility (Wilson et al. 2015), and links to criminal thinking (Tangney et al. 2017). In this study "criminal thinking" refers to "criminogenic cognitions," which are defined as thought patterns used to reduce the dissonance between moral standards and behaviour, rationalise deviant behaviour, and minimise negative consequences.

Finally, in one of the most comprehensive studies of meditation phenomena to date, Jared Lindahl, Willoughby Britton and colleagues

(2017: 1) investigated meditation-related experiences that are normally underreported: "particularly experiences that are described as challenging, difficult, distressing, functionally impairing, and/or requiring additional support." The authors employed a mixed-methods approach that included qualitative interviews with Western Buddhist meditation practitioners and experts from the Theravada, Zen, and Tibetan traditions. From this study the authors were able to delineate fifty-nine meditation-related experiences across seven domains: cognitive, perceptual, affective, somatic, conative, sense of self, and social. Whether a meditation-related experience was interpreted by the experiencer as adverse depended on a number of influencing factors related to the meditation practitioner and their practice, relationships, and health behaviours.

The dark night project

The use of the term "dark night" to refer to a variety of meditation adverse effects in research studies—and then in popular culture—can be traced to Professor Willoughby Britton, a meditation researcher who founded the "Dark Night Project" at Brown University. The Dark Night Project began as an effort to document, analyse, and publicise accounts of the adverse effects of meditation (Rocha 2014). In media interviews Britton (e.g. 2011a and 2011b) has reported that in addition to the above research studies, there exist numerous anecdotal reports of meditators in both clinical and non-clinical populations experiencing psychological and physical disturbances that appear to be directly related to meditation. Some of these instances were severe enough to require medication and hospitalisation and many were serious enough to have become a clinical problem that lasted, on average, for more than three years.

According to an article in *The Atlantic* titled "The Dark Knight of the Soul:"

> One of her [Britton's] team's preliminary tasks—a sort of archeological literature review—was to pore through the written canons of Theravadin, Tibetan, and Zen Buddhism, as well as texts within Christianity, Judaism, and Sufism. "Not every text makes clear reference to a period of difficulty on the contemplative path," Britton says, "but many did."
>
> "There is a sutta," a canonical discourse attributed to the Buddha or one of his close disciples, "where monks go crazy and commit suicide after doing contemplation on death," says Chris Kaplan,

a visiting scholar at the Mind & Life Institute who also works with Britton on the Dark Night Project.

Nathan Fisher, the study's manager, condenses a famous parable by the founder of the Jewish Hasidic movement. Says Fisher, "[the story] is about how the oscillations of spiritual life parallel the experience of learning to walk, very similar to the metaphor Saint John of the Cross uses in terms of a mother weaning a child ... first you are held up by a parent and it is exhilarating and wonderful, and then they take their hands away and it is terrifying and the child feels abandoned" (Rocha 2014).

Britton also founded Cheetah House, which started as a non-profit semi-residential social service organisation, where people who had experienced meditation adverse effects could stay and recover. Now no longer a physical place, Cheetah House still exists as a non-profit organisation. Its website states:

> Cheetah House is a non-profit organization that provides information and resources about meditation-related difficulties to meditators-in-distress and providers or teachers of meditation-based modalities.
>
> **Mission**
> The overarching mission of Cheetah House is:
>
> - to improve the safety and efficacy of meditation training by providing evidence-based research on meditation-related difficulties, contraindications and boundary conditions
> - to provide information, support and community to meditators-in-distress
> - provide information and training to providers and teachers about meditation-related difficulties and how to best address them
>
> **Goals**
> Normally, it takes 17 years for research findings to reach the end user. Cheetah House aims to shorten the science-to-service gap by providing research about meditation-related difficulties directly to meditators-in-distress, clinicians, educators and meditation teachers and organizations.[15]

---

[15] *Cheetah House* website at https://www.cheetahhouse.org/. Accessed January 2020.

While Britton's Dark Night Project has since been renamed the Varieties of Contemplative Experience (VOCE)[16] and the Cheetah House website does not mention the term "dark night" (except in a section that contains meditator's personal stories), Britton's work on meditation adverse effects, and the media attention that it attracted, led to the creation of a dark night meme in postmodern Buddhist meditation culture. The term found resonance with both journalists and meditators, and mentions of the dark night can be found on meditation podcasts,[17] blogs,[18] discussion forums[19] and social media sites such as Reddit. Within these contexts the dark night is used as an umbrella term to refer to any disturbing meditation-related phenomena or adverse effect, including experiences of depression, anxiety, dissociation, psychosis, or the re-experiencing of trauma.

Britton's work on meditation adverse effects has also inspired more research into meditation-related difficulties (in particular, the relationship between meditation and trauma) and an increased recognition of the wide diversity of meditation-related experiences. While Kornfield's earlier work on the dark night was therapeutically oriented, Britton's work is both therapeutically and politically oriented, as it has expanded the definition of the dark night to include symptoms (e.g. psychosis, re-traumatisation) that some modern meditation teachers have perhaps too quickly and rather insensitively dismissed as psychopathology—what Britton has referred to as victim blaming. Whereas in the past, people experiencing these types of severe symptoms have for the most part been simply excluded from meditation retreats and referred on to medical practitioners, there now seems to be more focus on understanding and integrating such experiences within meditation communities.

To summarise, the term "dark night" has a long history in Christian mysticism and a rather short history in Buddhist postmodernism. While the term has recently gained popularity in contemporary Western

---

[16] *The Varieties of Contemplative Experience* at https://www.brown.edu/research/labs/britton/research/varieties-contemplative-experience. Accessed July 2019.

[17] For example, *Buddhist Geeks*, "The Dark Side of Dharma," at https://art19.com/shows/buddhist-geeks/episodes/bb6cd056-ca75-42e0-bead-2d8d862aa46f. Accessed July 2019. Also, *Buddhist Geeks*, "The Dark Night Project," at https://art19.com/shows/buddhist-geeks/episodes/7c66e68d-ab9b-4a08-a21a-caa8d8a724f9. Accessed July 2019.

[18] For example, Ron Crouch, "The Bright Side of the Dark Night," at https://alohadharma.com/2015/03/03/the-bright-side-of-the-dark-night/. Accessed July 2019.

[19] *Dharma Overground* website at https://www.dharmaoverground.org/. Accessed July 2019.

meditation-based convert Buddhist lineages, its usage has been so vague as to be meaningless outside of the context of specific meditation teachers, traditions, and worldviews. The aim of this chapter has been to delineate the dark night; that is, to reach a more informed understanding of the various discourses surrounding the term. It is clear that the three dominant dark night discourses, while appearing quite dissimilar, do share a common theme; that is, they all attempt to differentiate between meditation-related difficulties and Western psychopathology. I have not attempted to discuss whether this differentiation is possible, however given that Buddhist postmodernism and modern Western psychology have co-arisen and been mutually informed by one another, it is likely to be a difficult task. Nevertheless, I believe it is a worthwhile task and I am hopeful that this book will inspire new avenues of thought regarding Buddhism, meditation adverse effects, and the dark night.

CHAPTER THREE

From enlightenment to symptom relief and personal transformation

> Thus, my point is that meditation is no panacea—it is strongly indicated in some cases, mildly in others, and clearly contraindicated in others. The precise guidelines for these discriminations have yet to be worked out.
>
> —Arnold A. Lazarus.[20]

Meditation as a western therapeutic intervention

The attempt to extract the common characteristics of "meditation" from a variety of religious traditions in order to come up with a generic definition is a uniquely modern Western phenomenon (Murphy and Donovan 1999: 2). As mentioned earlier, in religious traditions the term meditation does not refer to one distinct technique; rather it is an umbrella term that refers to a variety of practices that are intended to cultivate a particular state of being, and that promote self-transformation along a path defined in religious terms. Despite the huge variety of different religious meditation techniques and

---

[20] A.A. Lazarus, "Meditation: The Problems of Any Unimodal Technique," in *Meditation: Classic and Contemporary Perspectives*, eds. D.H. Shapiro, Jr and R.N. Walsh, 2009: 691.

traditions, all point towards a common goal; that is, if an individual practises meditation with dedication, for a prolonged period of time, it should eventually lead to a state of enlightenment; this is the primary goal of religious meditation.

For example, schools of Hinduism and Buddhism view meditation as a practice that has both short-term (state) and long-term (trait) transformational goals. However, unlike in Western secular applications, the changes in short term state (e.g. calming of the mind) produced by Hindu and Buddhist meditation are cultivated as part of a much larger transformational aim: the realisation of enlightenment, or a fully transformed consciousness. These traditions consider the everyday state of consciousness and the conventional sense of a "self" to be inaccurate, limited, and the cause of human suffering. This suffering can be overcome by following a prescribed religious path that includes many components (including ethics, ritual, and renunciation), and of which meditation is a key ingredient.

In contrast, modern Western secular meditation is focused primarily on symptom relief and transformation of the private psychological self. This is largely because the popular conceptualisation of meditation in the West has been heavily influenced by its affiliation with various streams of psychology. The idea that meditation has therapeutic potential can be traced back to 1934 when eminent psychiatrist and psychoanalyst Carl Jung posited that Zen Buddhism and psychotherapy shared a common goal—that is, the alleviation of human suffering via psychological means—and that the Buddhist teacher and psychoanalyst fulfilled a similar role in facilitating an individual's healing (Fields 1992: 205). Since then there have been numerous attempts to link meditation with psychology, including the ideas that mystical experiences associated with meditation are therapeutic, and that meditation can enhance or even replace psychotherapy (e.g. Smith 2009 [1975]). Historically, almost every school of psychological thought has been used to support these claims, and working definitions of meditation have evolved alongside developments in psychology.

Meditation as a panacea

A key theme that emerges from the historical interaction between meditation and psychology is the view of meditation as a type of panacea: an exalted technique with a therapeutic potential that transcends conventional Western psychotherapy. This view can be traced back to the early dialogue between psychoanalysis and Buddhism, and in particular to psychologist Erich Fromm (1900–1980), who reformulated psychoanalytic theory to propose a more positive definition of health as "wellbeing," rather than just the absence of illness. While Freud's psychoanalysis was concerned with only one aspect of the unconscious—that which deals with psychopathology—Fromm argued for a humanistic psychoanalysis that went beyond symptom relief and included the full recovery of the unconscious. Informed by his correspondence with renowned Zen scholar Daisetz T. Suzuki (1870–1966) and his analysis of Zen Buddhism, Fromm believed that meditation could be used as a tool to aid psychotherapy in not just the elimination of neuroses, but the "more radical aim of a complete transformation of the person" (Fromm, Suzuki, and de Martino 1993 [1974]: 137). This perspective provided the basis of a Western conceptualisation of meditation that has proved to be enduring: the optimistic view of meditation as a technique that has the power to provide healing beyond traditional forms of psychotherapy.

Another reoccurring theme that has contributed to overly positive Western perceptions of meditation is the idea that there is something inherently healing about present moment "awareness:" a key state cultivated by meditation, and in particular mindfulness meditation. For example, Shapiro et al. (2006: 376) note that "attention has been suggested in the field of psychology as critical to the healing process." One recent critique of medical mindfulness goes so far as to argue that the mindfulness movement portrays failure to pay attention (i.e. lack of awareness) as the principal cause of disease: "The specific culprit is inattention to the present moment" (Barker 2014: 171). This focus on the healing power of attention is a theme that can be traced back to noted psychiatrist and Buddhist sympathiser Fritz Perls (1893–1970), the founder of Gestalt therapy, who claimed that "awareness—by and of itself—is curative" (cited in Walsh and Shapiro 2006: 231). Perls designed experiments in self-awareness which were intended to bring to consciousness the thoughts and bodily activities that were considered to be creating "unconscious blocks," resulting in psychopathology (Dryden and Still 2006: 12). Similarly, renowned psychologist Carl Rogers (1902–1987) defined psychologically healthy, fully functioning people as "allowing awareness to flow freely in and through their experiences" (cited in Walsh and Shapiro 2006: 231). Humanistic psychotherapists like Perls and Rogers saw personal transformation, rather than symptom relief, as the end result of successful therapy, and this was brought about through awareness and acceptance. Dryden and Still (2006: 14) posit that many humanistic psychotherapists were familiar with, and probably influenced by, Buddhist ideas, even though this is rarely spoken of explicitly in their theory or practice.

The idea that meditation can facilitate awareness in order to access human potentials that go beyond the levels currently recognised by conventional Western psychology (what Abraham Maslow [1971] called "the farther reaches of human nature") is an idea that developed further within transpersonal psychology. For example, theoretical psychologist Ken Wilber created a developmental model that spans the full spectrum of human growth from infancy to enlightenment. Within this model, the earlier levels refer to the developmental territory studied by conventional psychology, and the higher "transpersonal" levels of consciousness refer to developmental stages that can only be accessed via spiritual practices such as meditation (Wilber 1996: 75–77). A similar idea was developed by psychologist and meditation teacher Jack Engler, who argued that psychology and Buddhism map discrete stages of a single developmental sequence, which starts with lower stages of conventional development (the domain of psychotherapy) and leads to more subtle stages of contemplative development (the domain of Buddhism) (Engler 1986). Engler has since revised his theory regarding a linear developmental model, but still believes that Buddhist theory and meditation practice address a type and range of functioning and wellbeing that go beyond traditional Western clinical practice (Engler 2003a). This view that meditation is a technique that reaches beyond conventional psychotherapy can be found throughout the transpersonal psychology literature. For example, Epstein (1995: 130) describes Buddhism as something that "reaches beyond therapy, toward a farther horizon of self-understanding that is not ordinarily accessible through psychotherapy alone." Similarly, Goleman (1971: 4) writes: "I conceptualise meditation as a "meta-therapy:" a procedure that accomplishes the major goals of conventional therapy and yet has as its end state a change far beyond the scope of therapies … an altered state of consciousness."

While both transpersonal psychology and psychoanalysis have been criticised for lacking conceptual, evidentiary, and scientific rigour, contemporary Western psychology is now exploring the relationship between meditation and human potential through the current dominant paradigm of cognitive psychology, and in particular "positive psychology." Positive psychology is concerned with the study of human flourishing and examines topics such as flow, values, and character strengths and virtues. Both cognitive psychology and positive psychology are based on the premise that intentional effort can produce changes in psychological health. For example, Walsh and Shapiro (2006) discuss the potential of meditation to enhance sophisticated psychological capacities such as emotional intelligence, equanimity, moral maturity, and lucidity during both waking and sleeping states. Other recent studies have examined the effects of mindfulness meditation on empathy (Berry et al. 2018), compassion (Fulton 2018), prosocial behaviour (Luberto et al. 2018), and wellbeing (Brown et al. 2007).

Hence, one of the factors that has contributed to meditation adverse effects being overlooked in psychological and clinical settings is quite straightforward: meditation is seen as a highly successful therapeutic intervention, and successful therapeutic interventions are supposed to help, not harm. A close examination of the psychological and scientific literature reveals that where meditation adverse effects have occurred, two strategies have been used in order to "explain away" these effects. The first is that in psychotherapy, any difficulties that occur during meditation have generally been attributed to "normal" psychotherapeutic processes such as catharsis or "working through" issues (Parsons 2009: 205; Bogart 1991: 397). A similar strategy was employed in early TM studies, where negative effects associated with meditation were simply attributed to "unstressing," a term used by the Students International Meditation Society (SIMS, the parent organisation of TM) to describe an initial, transient process whereby the problem areas in the meditator's life are solved or "normalised" (Otis 2009 [1984]).[21] Similarly, Walsh and Shapiro (2006: 234), when discussing complications that can arise as the result of meditation practice, write that from a Western psychological perspective:

> growth at any stage can be challenging, but many challenges may be potentially therapeutic, and clinicians have therefore described them as, for example, "crises of renewal", "positive disintegration", "creative illness", and "spiritual emergencies".

---

[21] However, Otis (1984) found "unstressing" to be an inadequate explanation of adverse effects in TM, as his study found that it was *experienced* meditators, not novices, who experienced the most adverse effects.

While Western psychological views of growth and transformation entail change that will be experienced as difficult by many people, regardless whether it is initiated by meditation, it is important to note that the meditation adverse effects to which this book refers to are quite literal. The term adverse effects is not, in this particular context, simply a metaphor for the emotional discomfort involved in personal growth. It would be quite unusual, for example, to expect auditory hallucinations, involuntary movements, or psychosis to result from psychotherapy, yet these effects have all reportedly been associated with meditation (Britton 2011a, 2011b; Farias and Wikholm 2015: 150–51). Further, meditation adverse effects that are long lasting and functionally impairing are unlikely to be the result of a normal process of psychological growth as understood by Western psychology. Despite this, it seems that a common explanation for meditation adverse effects is that they are simply the result of psychological discomfort arising from the therapeutic process.

Secondly, in Western psychotherapeutic contexts, difficulties associated with meditation may be misattributed to the individual meditator. Willoughby Britton argues that when it comes to meditation adverse effects there have been various instances of "victim blaming" and a tendency to assume that any problems encountered with meditation are the meditator's fault (Harris 2017). This is a perspective that can also be found in the psychological literature. For example, religious studies scholar Jeffrey Kripal (2007: 138) writes that in the 1960s and 1970s, people who showed interest in various altered states of consciousness—such as those resulting from meditation—were routinely diagnosed by the Freudian-influenced medical establishment as displaying signs of mental disorder. Even relatively recently, psychologist John Suler (1993) has argued that people who are drawn to meditation display a range of psychological problems: "from a fear of autonomy and refusal to assume adult responsibility to issues concerning incapacity for intimacy and passivity/dependency needs" (cited in Parsons 2009: 201). Other scholars have argued that in some situations meditation may be used as a form of "spiritual bypassing"—a technique used by individuals to avoid dealing with unresolved emotional issues or unfinished developmental and psychosocial tasks (Masters 2010)—and that people with identity and self-esteem problems are particularly attracted to meditation practice (Engler 1986).

However, this seems unlikely given the overwhelming global popularity of meditation today. Simply blaming adverse effects on the meditator is both an intellectually lazy and unhelpful practice, as it is likely that most meditation adverse effects involve a complex interaction between the practice of meditation and the individual meditator. However, in therapeutic contexts, where meditation is used to treat a variety of conditions that affect mood and cognition, it can be challenging to identify what difficulties are due to pre-existing or latent psychopathology and what might be caused by the meditation technique itself.

The relaxation response

One of the first theories that attempted to explain the effectiveness of meditation in clinical settings was that meditation helps produce a state of relaxation. Certain physiological changes have been consistently reported during meditation studies, including reduced heart rate, decreased oxygen consumption and carbon dioxide elimination, decreased blood pressure, increased skin resistance, and increased regularity and amplitude of alpha brain waves (e.g. Shapiro and Walsh 2009). As these physiological signs are typical responses that occur during relaxation, early researchers hypothesised that meditation produces a "wakeful hypometabolic state" of relaxation, and in 1975 cardiologist Herbert Benson coined the term "relaxation response" to describe the physiological and psychological effects that occur during meditation (Benson 1975). The attainment of a relaxation response during meditation has been replicated by many subsequent studies, and as a result, meditation practices are often reduced to and equated with (particularly in the popular media) other relaxation techniques, such as hypnosis, progressive relaxation, guided imagery, and biofeedback.

Today, the relaxation view of meditation has been recognised by scholars as overly reductionist and incomplete. Notably, Jon Kabat-Zinn changed the name of his mindfulness program from Stress Reduction and Relaxation Program to Mindfulness-Based Stress Reduction (MBSR) and removed the word "relaxation" from audiotapes and handouts. However, the association between meditation and relaxation has prevailed. Scholars have argued that this is because defining meditation as a relaxation technique allows it to fit more easily into secular therapeutic paradigms. For example, Gordon Boals posited that the relaxation view of meditation initially gained popularity because it demystified meditation and divorced it from its Eastern religious roots, "thereby countering the apparent secrecy and cultishness that have risen around most meditation procedures" (Boals 1978: 149). When reconceptualised as relaxation, meditation became more familiar, acceptable, and accessible to the scientific community.

However, one of the problems that arises when meditation is equated with relaxation is that it leads to unrealistically positive expectations regarding meditation outcomes. For example, a common popular misperception about meditation is that it always leads to the attainment of blissful states or the transcendence of one's day-to-day reality (Lustyk et al. 2009: 26). Perceptions such as this contribute to the view of meditation as a panacea and possibly result in the under-reporting of meditation adverse effects by practitioners. When meditation is presented as a harmless relaxation technique, this creates a situation that meditators may be reluctant to question or challenge, and they may be afraid to speak up regarding difficulties with practice. For example, Farias and Wikholm (2016) describe the case of a meditator who:

> tried out a mindfulness course because he was having some trouble falling asleep. While doing the course he became aware of negative thoughts, which wouldn't disappear no matter how much he accepted and tried to "let them go." After eight weeks his anxiety levels had increased from something barely noticeable to an everyday problem which he found hard to manage. "Is it my fault?" he wanted to know—and this is a common question for those who don't feel the wellbeing, relaxation, happiness kick one might expect to get when meditating. Let's not add stigmatisation to the list of adverse effects. It is no one's fault when meditation goes wrong.

Hence, meditators who do not experience relaxation, or worse, experience adverse effects, may attribute these experiences to their own perceived inadequacies as practitioners and be reluctant to speak up. Contributing to this effect is the fact that even in Western secular contexts it is common for meditators to practise in silence in order to enhance the deepening of concentration and awareness (Compson 2014). Limiting social interaction and encouraging uninterrupted practice may create conditions that contribute to meditators' reticence to speak about adverse effects with teachers. For example, it is possible that the common instruction in therapeutic mindfulness practice to "just sit with it" may create an implicit pressure on the meditator to endure any adverse effects in silence, leading to an under-reporting of adverse effects.[22]

Additionally, while it is true that some meditation practices may lead to states of tranquillity and relaxation, others may lead to states that are challenging or unpleasant. For example, the goal of mindfulness meditation as defined by Kabat-Zinn is to pay attention, on purpose, in the present moment, non-judgementally, and according to this definition, meditation may include paying attention to experiences that are challenging or unpleasant. Further, some scholars have warned against the blanket application of relaxation techniques, including meditation, as some people appear to have a paradoxical stress response to relaxation techniques, despite diligent attempts at training. This is referred to in the literature as "relaxation-induced anxiety" and is defined as a sudden increase in anxiety during deep relaxation that can range from mild to moderate intensity and that can approach the level of a minor panic episode (Lazarus and Mayne 1990).

Despite this, the relaxation view of meditation has greatly influenced the way in which scientific studies report the effects of meditation. Scholars have argued that studies of meditation may emphasise or de-emphasise certain effects in order to fit within acceptable modern paradigms, such as that of Western therapeutic culture (Britton et al. 2013). So far, studies of meditation have emphasised its relaxation effects; however, the evidence that meditation can lead to a state of relaxation is based primarily on studies of only two types of meditation: TM, and mindfulness techniques derived from the Theravada stream of Buddhism. Interestingly, a number of studies exist that show that other forms of meditation, such as those from the Vajrayana and Hindu Tantric traditions, produce a state of arousal, not relaxation. For example, a study by Amihai and Kozhevnikov (2014) suggests that different types of meditation are based on different neurophysiological mechanisms, which give rise to either a relaxation or arousal response.

An interdisciplinary review by Britton et al. (2013) also lends support to meditation's arousing effects, providing further evidence that the common characterisation of meditation as a relaxation technique is incomplete. The evidence from this review suggests that not only

---

[22] From a psychoanalytic perspective, meditation can be problematic if it causes unconscious material to arise into consciousness, and then this conscious content is simply observed (as meditation advises) and not worked-through (Parsons 2009; Bogart 1991).

do different types of meditation techniques lead to either relaxation or arousal, but that paradoxical arousal effects may occur even with meditation techniques that were traditionally thought to be relaxing. Specifically, some types of Buddhist meditation (e.g. *vipassana*) can actually result in increased wakefulness and lower sleep propensity depending on the dose and the expertise of the practitioner. As meditation adverse effects are by definition arousing and not relaxing, research studies that focus only on the relaxing effects of meditation risk ignoring other categories of phenomenological experience that may include adverse effects.

Issues of self and non-self

Attempts to integrate meditation into Western psychotherapy have focused on the therapeutic benefits of meditation as a technique to help a person address psychopathology and develop a healthy sense of self. Secular meditation-based therapies are therefore concerned with individuals and their adjustment to their social context, which scholar Geoffrey Samuel describes as "deeply invested by the Western sense of the separate individual" (Samuel 2015: 494). Yet, contemporary therapeutic meditation practices such as mindfulness and TM derive from modernist versions of Buddhism and Hinduism, which emphasise the deconstruction of the individual self, or the realisation of non-self. In Hinduism this is referred to as self-realisation (*atma-jnana*) and is equated with knowledge of the true self beyond identification with material phenomena. Similarly, Buddhism denies the existence of the sense of self (*atman*) as a stable and continuous entity. Samuel (2015: 494) writes: "For Buddhists, the human sense of oneself as a coherent, stable individual is ultimately artificial and mistaken ... This is not an optional extra for Buddhists; it is a central assertion of the tradition." Thus, in these religious traditions, meditation is seen as a technique that can aid in the desirable realisation that the conventional sense of self is an illusion. For example, highly valued meditative attainments such as *satori* and *kenshō* are associated with significant changes in sense of self.

This presents an interesting challenge for Western therapeutic meditation with its current individualistic orientation. While the Western meditation literature describes a helpful shift in perspective that arises from basic mindfulness practice, the idea of non-self as defined by Buddhism fits poorly into the contemporary Western therapeutic context, which focuses on the fulfilment of the individual's personal desires and the gratification of the psychological self. Further, the contemporary psychological self is the product of the last three or four hundred years of Western civilisation; scholars have argued that the concept of an independent and autonomous selfhood was unknown in the Buddha's day. Others have argued that the modern Western conceptualisation of the self as a unique individual is foreign to traditional Asian cultures. There is evidence to suggest that Asian cultures do differ from Western cultures in that they are more collectively oriented and less concerned with individuality (e.g. Triandis 1989). Therefore, it is possible these cultures may find teachings of non-self easier to integrate, and that insights of non-self associated with meditation may present unique challenges to contemporary Western individuals who have a strong sense of separate personal identity.

Regardless of whether the Buddha recognised a private psychological self in the same way that we do today, a major problem arises because in Western therapeutic approaches, meditation is seen simply as a technique whereby "one's old notion of self can better get what it wants" (Rosch 1999: 222). However, as a contemplative practice, the goal of meditation is not self-gratification or self-fulfilment, but rather the deconstruction of the self. While psychotherapy seeks to modify the self, the original goal of meditation in a religious context is to experience a consciousness beyond the cognitive structures and constructs of the conventional self. For example, Bogart (1991) argues that while Western psychology values identity constancy and the formation of a stable and solid sense of self, from the Buddhist perspective this represents a point of arrested development; in Buddhism such self-coherency is achieved in order to be transcended.

That Western psychotherapy and the Eastern religions from which contemporary forms of meditation originate have fundamentally different ideas regarding the self is a fact that has been largely ignored in the scientific literature on meditation. It is possible this is because there is an implicit assumption that both psychotherapy and the contemplative traditions share a common goal—the alleviation of human suffering—and that traditional ideas regarding non-self are seen as irrelevant in contemporary secular pursuits of this goal. While this may be true to an extent, the definition of "suffering" differs significantly according to context. In modern Western psychology, suffering is something that is *experienced by the self*. In Buddhist and Hindu traditions, suffering is *caused by the illusion of the individual self*.[23] For example, in Buddhist philosophy, any relief from suffering that is provided by an attempt to adapt to external conditions—arguably the goal of most forms of psychotherapy—would be temporary; true alleviation of suffering would only come from realising the illusory nature of the self. As C.W. Huntington Jr. (2018) writes:

> Both Buddhism and psychotherapy are directed toward the problem of human suffering, but *nibbana*—the goal of Theravada Buddhist practice—and the therapeutic goal of "mental health" are grounded in two distinct understandings of the nature and scope of human suffering. While psychotherapy aims at the alleviation of symptoms experienced as extrinsic or peripheral to the patient's underlying core sense of self, Buddhism addresses a form of suffering (*dukkha*) considered intrinsic to the experience of the personal self as an independent agent defined by its capacity to analyse and think, to judge, choose, act and be acted upon. Buddhist teachings associate these two forms of suffering with two distinct but interrelated truths about the self and its world: the first is "conventional" truth (*sammutisacca*), which governs day-to-day, practical affairs, where appearances are all that matters; and the second is "ultimate" or "absolute" truth (*paramatthasacca*), which reveals the illusory nature of these same appearances.
>
> The practice of psychotherapy is, accordingly, dedicated to a method of healing that leaves the conventional structure of self-as-agent intact as the focal point of attention, whereas Buddhist spiritual practice engages in a sustained, methodical dismantling of our customary preoccupation with self-centered experience.

---

[23] Asian meditation teachers such as Mahasi Sayadaw and the current Dalai Lama have admitted to being surprised by the unfamiliar psychological problems they find in Western meditation students. Mahasi Sayadaw has referred to psychological problems as a new form of *dukkha*, one that he termed "psychological suffering." Similarly, the Dalai Lama was reportedly surprised to hear that Western students suffer from self-hatred, as there is no equivalent Tibetan concept matching this psychological issue. Hence, there seems to be a categorical difference between Western conceptions of psychological suffering and Buddhist conceptions of suffering. However, there is evidence to suggest that depression, anxiety and psychosis exist in Tibetan cultures and hence these types of claims must be scrutinised and should not be taken at face value.

This key difference in definitions of suffering may be another factor contributing to meditation adverse effects being overlooked in secular therapeutic contexts.[24] That is, secular therapeutic forms of meditation may induce effects that go beyond symptom relief; specifically, changes to the meditator's sense of a stable individual self. To use the words of Huntington Jr., secular therapeutic meditation may not always leave the "self-as-agent" intact. A review of the psychological literature shows support for this idea, and also indicates that such experiences of insight into the impermanent nature of the self during meditation may be extremely challenging. For example, in his pioneering phenomenological study of insight meditation practitioners, Jack Kornfield (1979: 54) describes the challenging aspect of non-self experiences in *vipassana* meditation:

> Deep practice also involves mindfulness of death-like experiences, reported as feeling a dying of the body, death of illusions, of self-images, of ideals, of past and future, and the idea of one self as permanent or solid at all. One of the experiences most commonly described as powerful or transformative is the insight into the moment-to-moment changing nature of the self. Students report experiencing themselves as simply a flowing process of sense perceptions and reactions, with no sense of a fixed self or person existing apart from this process at all.

Similarly, Jack Engler (2003b: 92–93) writes:

> Discovering that there is no ontological core to consciousness or self that is independent and enduring and no stable "objects" of perception ... no "I" or "thing" enduring across the gap between one construction and arising of the next—this is a profound shock. It is experienced as a free fall into a looking-glass world where, as the Mad Hatter tells Alice, "Things are not as they seem!" It so turns our normal sense of self and reality on its head that, as Niels Bohr

---

[24] This definitional issue is also reflected in the ideological split between Joseph Goldstein and Jack Kornfield. Goldstein argues that the highest Buddhist aim of liberation from suffering has been replaced by more humanistic psychological concerns. He writes: "I see a tendency to let go of that goal and become satisfied with something less: doing good in the world, having more harmonious relationships, seeking a happier life. That's all beautiful but in my view it misses the essential point" (Gleig 2012: 136).

once remarked about quantum physics … if you don't get dizzy thinking about it, you haven't understood it.

A recent study by Lomas et al. (2015) also reports on the difficulties that meditators can encounter with non-self experiences. When describing one participant's experience, the authors note: "the deconstruction of the self (which is the goal of the practice) was experienced as a frightening dissolution of identity, rather than as a sense of liberation (which the practice is arguably designed to invoke)" (Lomas et al. 2015: 855). Other participants in the study described their non-self experiences as disorienting, frightening, alienating, and disturbing. Sean Pritchard's (2016: 66) qualitative study of *vipassana* meditators also supports these findings, with one participant describing an insight into non-self as a "death experience."

Further, Andrea Grabovac (2015) argues that some participants in secular mindfulness-based interventions appear to progress through the Theravadan Buddhist stages of insight, even during a relatively short period of time, such as an eight-week MBSR program. This progress involves experiences that can be extremely psychologically challenging and that may become clinically significant—including experiences of non-self. Hence, it seems that even when secularised and applied in Western therapeutic contexts, meditation may cause the concept of a stable, permanent psychological self to be challenged, and this may result in adverse effects.

Mourning the loss of the self

The "sense of self" is construed in multiple ways. Research from cognitive science suggests that the sense of self is comprised of multiple processes and it is not yet well understood which changes in self-related processing are expected, intended, or achievable through meditation (Lindahl and Britton 2019: 158). In their recent paper *"I Have This Feeling of Not Really Being Here": Buddhist Meditation and Changes in Sense of Self* Lindahl and Britton (2019) reported six discrete changes in sense of self as described by Buddhist meditators: change in narrative self, loss of sense of ownership, loss of sense of agency, change in sense of embodiment, change in self-other or self-world boundaries, and loss of sense of basic self. These changes in sense of self were reported as either transient or long-lasting, positive or distressing, enhancing or impairing. The meditators in the study also related various interpretations of these changes, ranging from insights associated with Buddhist doctrines to psychopathologies such as depersonalisation. Overall, the study found that more global changes in sense of self (such as those related to a loss of basic sense of self) were associated with higher levels of distress and impairment.

The study contains numerous comments from meditation practitioners that illustrate some of the challenges inherent to changes in sense of self. For example, in one case the change was described as a complete loss of personal and narrative identity that started during a meditation retreat and continued into daily life:

> But on the inside, I was deeply wounded in the sense of my identity. I felt that my identity was threatened. I would walk, and I would feel that I forgot my past. At some point on the retreat, I literally forgot my name. I was like, "Wait, what is my name again?" Yeah, I totally forgot. [...] I would look at other people and interact with people, and they would say regular things like, "Oh, I like that type of ice cream" or "Oh, I like that thing." And I remember hearing that, and I'm like: "Wait, how do you know that? How do you know what you like and dislike? How do you know who you are?" It was like I couldn't figure out who I was, what I like, or who I am. I felt like I had no identity (Britton and Lindahl 2019: 164).

Another example illustrates how a loss of narrative self and personal identity might impact motivation and drive:

> It basically felt like whatever personality I thought I had before just disintegrated. And it wasn't an expansive disintegration into unity or bliss or anything like that. It was a disintegration into dust. And I really had the feeling of being in a very, very, very narrow, small, limited psychological space. [...] I didn't believe in all the things that people do to tell themselves that "something is worth it" or "just be you"—all those positive psychological frameworks that people use to get through life just seemed really unconvincing. [...] I came to this conclusion during that time period that personality is just a structure without any real substance to it. And I don't know if that really solved anything for me or resolved anything for me. [...] But I was just convinced that there wasn't any point in working on this structure (Britton and Lindahl 2019: 164).

Hence, while it may be the goal of traditional meditation practice, a loss of sense of self may also be experienced negatively, particularly when it relates to a loss of a basic sense of self or personal identity. This may be understandably exacerbated for secular meditation practitioners who were not actively seeking or expecting this effect. For example, I have had a number of personal conversations with individuals who experienced an unexpected loss of sense of self as a result of meditation. Several described this experience as being akin to "seeing something and then being unable to un-see it." Some used the term "dissociation" to describe their experience and at least one individual expressed a desire to "go back to how things were before [meditation]."

Even for meditators who do desire a fundamental change in sense of self, the realisation of non-self as defined by religious traditions may still involve an unexpected and challenging aspect: grief regarding the loss of the "conventional self." For example, Parsons (2009: 202) argues:

> We repress the fact of an unconstructed non-core to existence. If the therapeutic task can be conceived along the lines of mourning, the psychoanalytic encounter with Buddhism now reveals the need to work-through an even deeper level of mourning: that of the existence of a continuous, stable, enduring self.

Here we must ask an important question: is the loss of a continuous, stable, enduring self a desirable or healthy goal? For ascetics and renunciates, maybe. But for the average person living in modern society, with relationships and responsibilities, the self serves an important purpose. Beyond the more obvious pragmatic functions of having a sense of embodiment or a sense of agency, there are also benefits to having a conceptual, autobiographical sense of self and a coherent personal narrative. Narrative identity theory posits that individuals form an identity by integrating their life experiences into an internalised, evolving story of the self that provides the individual with a sense of unity, purpose and meaning (McAdams and McLean 2013). Scholars have argued that individuals who have a strong sense of a personal narrative experience greater wellbeing and are better buffered against existential threat (e.g. Sedikides, Wildschut, and Baden, 2004; Routledge and Arndt, 2005). Therefore it is not correct to assume, as many proponents of meditation do, that a reduction in self-related processing *will always* result in improved mental health and wellbeing. The research (e.g. Lindahl and

Britton 2019) does not support this idea; rather it highlights the importance of delineating *which* specific aspect of self is the target for transformational change.

In sum, it is clear that while Western psychotherapy and meditation share some similar goals and functions in the enhancement of individual wellbeing, there are also major philosophical differences that must be acknowledged. Some scholars have gone so far as to argue that the Buddhist and Hindu goal of meditation (the realisation that the individual self is illusory) is fundamentally irreconcilable with the Western therapeutic goal of facilitating the development of a cohesive psychological self (Bradwejn, Dowdall, and Iny 1985). Others have argued that a more balanced approach may be to maintain a clear distinction between the goals of Western psychotherapy and the goals of Eastern meditation, and to admit the differences between the stated aims of each technique (Bacher 1981). While the idea of completely excluding meditation from psychotherapy seems extreme, the literature suggests that in modern contexts it would also be impossible to make a clear distinction between "Western psychotherapy" and "Eastern meditation," because they have co-arisen and developed in a mutually informing way. Hence, it is up to secular clinicians and meditation teachers to recognise that non-self experiences may occur, even with secular meditation, and that these experiences are distinct from psychopathology. Further, future research should continue to investigate the various aspects of self-related processing and how these relate to meditation.

Meditation research methods

A final factor to consider is that the scientific study of meditation has occurred primarily in clinical trials and self-report surveys that have focused on quantitative, bio-neurological investigations into the effects of meditation. While clinical trials are the most reliable method for acquiring accurate information about the effects of meditation, their design does not specifically seek to test for side effects or adverse effects. Currently there is no standard method for identifying adverse effects in clinical trials, and the vast majority (>75%) of meditation studies do not actively assess adverse effects, but rely on participants to spontaneously self-report any negative experiences that occur (Lindahl et al. 2017). However, research into the nature of self-report has demonstrated that participants in clinical trials are unlikely to spontaneously volunteer information about negative experiences due to the influence of social desirability effects and demand characteristics. Therefore it is probable that the prevalence of adverse effects in clinical trials, including meditation studies, is greatly underreported. Indeed, Lindahl et al. (2017) posit that passive monitoring of adverse effects in clinical trials may underestimate their prevalence by more than twenty-fold.

Additionally, as quantitative studies de-emphasise the subjective experience of participants, very little research exists on the "lived experience" of meditators, resulting in a skewed and incomplete perspective that focuses mainly on the positive effects of meditation. The small number of qualitative research studies on meditation that do exist indicate that there is a comprehensive phenomenology of meditation experiences that commonly includes negative effects. For example, Jack Kornfield's (1979) mixed methods study of meditators during a three-month *vipassana* retreat reported several adverse effects including intense negative emotions, involuntary movements, abnormal somatic sensations, and altered state experiences. More recently, a qualitative study by Lomas et al. (2015) found that one quarter of participants encountered substantial difficulties with meditation, including troubling thoughts and feelings which were hard to manage, exacerbation of depression and anxiety, and in two cases, psychosis requiring hospitalisation.

Additionally, Sean Pritchard (2016) examined the qualitative experience of advanced *vipassana* meditators and found that disturbing emotions such as anger, fear, anxiety, and shame often occurred during certain stages of meditation practice, along with challenging shifts in perception of self. Finally, Burrows (2016: 285), in describing her small ($n = 13$) qualitative pilot study of young adult mindfulness meditators, writes:

> the finding that many of the 13 participants had negative or unusual experiences raises a more fundamental issue—why is it that such an unusually high number of participants experienced negative emotions in this study and not in the vast majority of randomized controlled trials? Obviously, better controlled research is clearly needed to tease out whether the findings in this preliminary, uncontrolled study are unique to this study or generalizable to other mindfulness-based interventions.

These qualitative studies suggest that meditation adverse effects may in fact be a common and normal part of meditation practice that is being overlooked in clinical studies. It is worth noting that meditation-related adverse effects have also been reported in clinical and medical case reports, including descriptions of meditation-induced psychosis (Kuijpers et al. 2007), depersonalisation (Kennedy 1976), de-repression of trauma (Treleaven 2010), and mania (Yorston 2001). However, as case reports are concerned with single instances they are often regarded as unscientific and less worthy of consideration. While case reports are of course not as scientifically rigorous as randomised control trials, they are still a key mode of transmitting knowledge and have played a significant role in the evolution of academic psychology and psychotherapy in the area of religious and spiritual issues (e.g. Lukoff et al. 1999). Scholars have argued that case reports have an important epistemological function, as over time they accumulate into a body of knowledge which then guides clinical practice and suggests where research should turn to next. For example, Hunter (1986) writes: "they [case studies] are frequently the as-yet-unorganised evidence at the forefront of clinical medicine." Therefore it would appear that case reports on meditation, while sparse in quantity and less scientifically rigorous than clinical trials, do lend support to the idea that meditation adverse effects exist and are worthy of further investigation.

A final point worth considering is that an overly positive view of meditation may have developed within Western psychology because a large number of influential psychologists and researchers were, and continue to be, meditation practitioners themselves: what Parsons (2009: 199) terms "cultural insiders" and David McMahan (2008: 28–30) refers to as "Buddhist sympathisers." Certainly, many authors who have written significant studies of Buddhist meditation and psychology (for example, Jack Engler, Mark Epstein, Paul Cooper, Jeffrey Rubin, Jeremy Safran, Jack Kornfield, Joseph Goldstein, and Jon Kabat-Zinn, to name a few) represent a baby boomer generation who were attracted to Eastern religions, went on meditation retreats, worked closely with gurus, and then integrated meditation practices into their own therapeutic work. In *Mindful America*, Wilson (2014: 33) notes that most early MBSR instructors were Buddhists, or directly involved in formal Buddhist meditation practice. Similarly, Lopez Jr (2008: 209–210) argues that the scientific study of Buddhist meditation is so popular compared to meditation techniques from other religious traditions because of the "religious predilections of the researchers involved." A similar situation can be found with TM, with Walsh and Shapiro (2006: 230) noting that many of the early TM studies were published by "enthusiastic advocates using self-selected subjects."[25]

Unfortunately, throughout the history of science, some researchers have selectively interpreted or ignored data that fails to confirm a favoured research hypothesis. This is commonly described as a confirmation bias, and "connotes the seeking or interpreting of evidence in ways that are partial to existing beliefs, expectations, or a hypothesis in hand" (Nickerson 1998: 175). While rigorous experimental design and the peer review system aim to minimise this type of bias, there is evidence that it still exists in the peer review process (Emerson et al. 2010) and in academic psychology (Hergovich, Schott, and Berger 2010). There is also evidence to suggest that the confirmation bias may be especially harmful to objective evaluations of nonconforming results, and that data that conflict with the researcher's expectations may be rejected as unreliable, producing the "file drawer problem" where undesirable results are simply filed away and forgotten (Rosenthal 1979). In the case of meditation studies, such bias may lead to the under-reporting of adverse effects. While standards of meditation research have improved considerably since the early TM studies, questions still remain regarding the objectivity of researchers who are also ardent supporters of the meditation practices they study. In particular, it is important to consider whether conflicts of interest or expectancy effects might be contributing to an overly positive view of meditation that overlooks potential adverse effects.

---

[25] However, it must be noted that many supporters of meditation do also recognise its limits. For example, Kornfield (1993b) argues that for most people meditation does not "do it all" and there are areas (such as grief, fear and phobias) where Western therapy is a much quicker and more successful intervention than meditation. Kornfield also recognises that some psychological issues that arise at retreats cannot be resolved simply by meditating. In *A Path With Heart*, he notes that at least half of the Western students who undertake three-month *vipassana* retreats at the Insight Meditation Society are unable to continue with practice because they encounter so many emotional and psychological issues.

CHAPTER FOUR

Making meditation secular: meditation as a detachable technique

> *Paradoxically, while meditation is often considered the heart of Buddhism, it is also deemed the element most detachable from the tradition itself ... More than any other facet of Buddhism, meditation and mindfulness are presented as psychological, spiritual, or scientific techniques rather than as religious practices.*
> —David L. McMahan.[26]

"Secular" meditation

A large part of the appeal of popular mainstream forms of meditation is that they are usually presented as being secular, or unassociated with any formal religion. While in contemporary religious studies the term "religion" is viewed as problematic and vague, a distinction is commonly made between what is "religious" and what is "secular." Secularism is differentially defined depending upon the context within which it is discussed; for example, secularism as a philosophy versus secularism as a political stance. However, broadly speaking, secularism is identified as a separation, and movement away, from religion. There is statistical

---

[26] D.L. McMahan, *The Making of Buddhist Modernism*, 2008: 185.

evidence of secularisation in almost all European countries since the end of World War II, a trend which has developed alongside modernisation (Habermas 2006: 2). While there is an active debate regarding whether secularisation has been happening or whether there has been a return of religion, or a turn towards "postsecular" themes, in the modern West secularism is a widely accepted paradigm. As a result, a growing number of people practise what is commonly described as secular meditation.

However, it is important to note that the distinction between secular and religious meditation is subjective. The only real way to differentiate between secular meditation and religious meditation is to focus on the end goal of the practice (that is, whether it is a religious goal or a non-religious goal), and on claims to secularity (that is, what different scholars, teachers, and religious practitioners have claimed about particular meditation practices and their end goals). For example, contemporary meditation teachers who apply mindfulness meditation in a purely clinical way might view mindfulness as secular because it is employed towards clinical goals, such as the alleviation of chronic pain. Likewise, the Transcendental Meditation technique created by Maharishi Mahesh Yogi claims to be secular because its goals are this-worldly, physiological, and health-related, and no adherence to a belief system is required in order for it to be effective—TM practitioners are free to follow any religion. The *vipassana* tradition could be said to exist on a spectrum of secularity, with claims to secularity varying according to the specific *vipassana* organisation. For example, the American organisation Spirit Rock is explicit regarding its connection to Buddhism, but it also draws on a number of other spiritual and psychological traditions and has what could be described as an East-meets-West integrative approach. The Insight Meditation Society is known for maintaining a more traditional approach and for being more conservative in terms of preserving their Theravada lineage (Gleig 2012).[27] Finally, *vipassana* in the tradition of S. N. Goenka claims to be completely non-religious and refers to its teaching as an "art of living." In general, *vipassana* meditation articulates a relatively secular approach to Buddhist philosophy and practice. As David Treleaven (2012: 78) notes:

> Judging by the infrequent number of times the word "enlightenment" appears in WVM [Western Vipassana Meditation] texts, it appears that most WVM teachers, while still drawing upon foundational

---

[27] Insight Meditation Society website, https://www.dharma.org/about-us/. Accessed December 2019.

teachings such as the Eightfold Path, deemphasize the term in lieu of secular values that can inform and improve the quality of one's life.

While these specific meditation practices are generally presented as secular, meditation is still widely considered by many leading figures in the field as a deeply spiritual practice and there has been much debate regarding whether meditation can ever be effectively separated from its religious origins (e.g. Arat 2017; Hale 2018; Sharf 2015). Some critics of secular meditation have noted that religious elements sometimes remain implicit even in clinical applications of meditation and there is much debate regarding whether mindfulness-based interventions are secular. For example, during an eight week MBSR course, participants learn Buddhist-derived practices such as *vipassana* meditation, walking meditation, and loving-kindness (*metta*) meditation. MBSR also promotes "choiceless awareness," a practice popularised by Eastern philosopher Jiddu Krishnamurti (1895–1986) (Hickey 2008). Similarly, in Acceptance and Commitment Therapy—a psychological intervention that uses mindfulness strategies—one of the goals is to make contact with a "transcendent sense of self." This notion of "transcendence" is similar to the teachings of Jnana Yoga and Advaita Vedanta, and of neo-Hindu gurus Bhagavan Sri Ramana Maharshi and Sri Nisargadatta Maharaj (Seiden and Lam 2010).

While an in-depth analysis of whether meditation can ever be truly secular is beyond the scope of this book, for present purposes it is useful to distinguish between secular meditation and religious meditation to the extent that it helps to identify a particular discourse, while also keeping in mind that the boundary between the secular and the religious is both arbitrary and porous. This book, for the most part, has narrowed its focus to three types of secular meditation: Transcendental Meditation (TM), mindfulness, and *vipassana*. These are the meditation practices that have been studied the most in Western clinical and research settings, and for which the most data exists. They are also the practices that are most commonly presented as secular. Other forms of meditation that are practised within the context of an organised religious tradition (for example, a school of Buddhism) will be referred to as "traditional meditation" or "religious meditation".

Meditation as a detachable technique

In contemporary Western culture, discussions about spiritual or religious issues are often seen as unscientific or problematic, possibly because there is little scientific understanding of how spirituality is related to the "hard sciences" (e.g. Walach 2015: 3). However, somewhat paradoxically, meditation techniques that have their origins in religious traditions are regularly being utilised in Western scientific and clinical settings. A key way that researchers and clinicians have attempted to resolve this apparent conflict is by viewing meditation as a "detachable" technique; that is, a technique that can be completely separated from its traditional religious context and re-purposed within a secular scientific paradigm. In the case of Buddhism, McMahan (2008) argues that the idea that meditation techniques can be isolated from their wider religious, ethical, social, and cosmological contexts was implicit in the nineteenth century and became explicit in Western discussions of meditation written in the mid-twentieth century. For example, in *The Making of Buddhist Modernism*, McMahan (2008: 185) cites Rear Admiral E. H. Shattock, a British naval officer who studied meditation in a Theravada monastery and who wrote in his 1958 book, *An Experiment in Mindfulness*: "Meditation ... is a really practical occupation: it is in no sense necessarily a religious one, though it is usually thought of as such. It is itself basically academic, practical, and profitable." More recently, Jon Kabat-Zinn, the founder of MBSR, was quoted in an interview with *TIME* magazine as saying: "Mindfulness is often spoken of as the heart of Buddhist meditation. It's not about Buddhism, but about paying attention. That's what all meditation is, no matter what tradition or particular technique is used" (Szalavitz 2012). Both of these comments are indicative of how meditation is now commonly viewed in the modern West; as a pragmatic and inherently secular tool that can be removed from its particular religious context and applied to a variety of practical worldly pursuits.

De-contextualisation: privileging meditation and marginalising religious context

One of the key ways that meditation has been detached and distanced from religion is via a process of de-contextualisation. This involves privileging meditation above other religious elements such as scripture, doctrine, and ritual, and marginalising the religious context that normally accompanies meditation practices. Interestingly, while meditation is often identified today in the West as an essential—if not, *the* essential—component of some Eastern religious practices, it has not always held this special status. In fact, historically, relatively few people have meditated (Braun 2013). McMahan (2008: 185) notes that in the contemporary West, meditation is popularly considered to be the "heart of Buddhism," however while meditation has always been considered essential to the Buddhist goal of enlightenment, only a small minority of monks and ascetics have practised meditation in a serious way. Prior to the colonial era, the majority of Buddhist monks did not meditate, but rather functioned as clerics and priests, engaged in scholarship or ritual, and acted as *punnakhetta* ("fields of merit" or recipients of charity) (Braun 2013: 3–6). Likewise, in Hindu traditions, meditation as distinct from other devotional activities such as *puja* or *kirtan* singing, was a fairly rare practice until the twentieth century Western middle class movements. The practice of postural yoga, which is closely linked to meditation, was also rare and mainly the domain of sadhus until the early twentieth century.

Even today, in most Eastern religions meditation is not a particularly common practice. For example, Buddhist studies scholar Robert Sharf (1995: 253) writes that in the Theravada tradition, few monks today expect to reach enlightenment in what is currently thought to be the degenerate third age of Buddhism, *Mappo*, or the Age of Dharma Decline. Hence, despite the impact of the *vipassana* movement, most Theravadan monks do not meditate, but rather specialise in teaching, scholarship or ritual, and spend their time cultivating moral virtue in the hope of being re-born in better circumstances. Most Theravada monks insist that the development of morality and observance of monastic rule is more essential than meditation (Sharf 1995: 241). Similarly, in the Korean Son tradition, only about five percent of the clergy practise meditation. In some circumstances provisions have been made for lay people to practise meditation, but generally it has been considered "an arduous endeavour taken up by a small number of monastics who specialise in contemplative practice" (McMahan 2008: 184). The current Western emphasis on meditation is therefore not necessarily reflective of how meditation has been viewed historically or even currently within traditions such as Buddhism.

There have been particular points in history where meditation has been prioritised above other religious elements and activities, and this has usually been related to laicisation. Sharf (2015) cites examples from eighth century Zen and Tibetan Dzogchen traditions, where meditation teachers replaced traditional forms of meditation with newer styles that were simple enough to be accessed by a lay audience. These new "democratised" meditation techniques were regarded as direct approaches to enlightenment that avoided the need for extensive training in concentration exercises (*samatha*), the attainment of advanced contemplative states (such as *jhana*), mastery of scripture, proficiency in ritual, or the renunciation of lay life. Sharf (2015: 476) notes that these Zen and Dzogchen reformers were:

> interested in developing a method simple enough to be accessible to those who were unschooled in Buddhist doctrine and scripture, who were not necessarily wedded to classical Indian cosmology, who may not have had the time or inclination for extended monastic practice, and who were interested in immediate results as opposed to incremental advancement over countless lifetimes.

In the case of Southeast Asian Buddhism, historical records suggest that meditation practice was rare until the colonial period. During this time the influential Burmese Buddhist monk Ledi Sayadaw (1846–1923) popularised the *vipassana* meditation technique as part of an effort to promote meditation amongst lay practitioners (Braun 2013). Like the earlier Zen and Dzogchen teachers, Ledi Sayadaw designed the *vipassana* technique as a way to standardise and simplify meditation, and make it widely accessible to a general lay audience who did not have the time or interest to participate in extensive religious training or ritual. While Ledi Sayadaw did not completely neglect Buddhist doctrine or morality, Braun (2018) argues that his popularisation of meditation did lead to "the elevation of the layperson's role in Buddhism and even laid the ground for meditation to detach from the rest of Buddhism as a separate tradition in its own right." However it is important to note that Ledi Sayadaw's privileging of meditation was done out of a sense of necessity; he believed that making the *vipassana* practice widely accessible would help to protect the Buddhist tradition from colonial threat. Hence Ledi Sayadaw's privileging of meditation was aimed at the preservation of the Buddhist tradition, not the secularisation of meditation techniques for non-religious purposes.

In contemporary Western culture, the prioritisation of meditation above other religious elements has also been associated with laicisation. In particular, the *vipassana* movement has gained popularity among lay practitioners and has had a significant influence on contemporary

Western meditation culture. Western teachers such as Joseph Goldstein, Jack Kornfield and Sharon Salzberg made this meditation technique particularly popular, and *vipassana* is one of the most commonly practiced styles of meditation in the West and one of the foundational practices of Buddhist modernism. *Vipassana* meditation is taught without most of the religious elements associated with Theravada Buddhism, does not require familiarity with religious philosophy, and can be taught in a relatively short period of time, usually in a ten-day retreat format.

Meditation has also been prioritised in other Western modernist versions of Buddhism, in particular, Japanese Zen. Scholars have argued that Western views of Zen have been disproportionately influenced by the writings of a small group of twentieth-century intellectuals, including D.T. Suzuki (1870–1966), Hisamatsu Shin'ichi (1889–1980) and Nishitani Keiji (1900–1990). These scholars promoted a rational, humanistic version of Zen that avoided ritual and was based on experience rather than faith. For example, in *The Making of Buddhist Modernism*, McMahan (2008) argues that D.T. Suzuki in particular encouraged the understanding of *zazen* as detachable from the ritual, liturgy, priesthood, and hierarchy of institutional Zen settings, and de-contextualised Zen literature in order to incorporate it into a framework of modern Western ideas. McMahan also writes at length about the Western cultural factors that have combined to create such a "meditation-friendly environment" in the West; that is, a culture that is particularly receptive to the privileging of meditation.

The privileging of meditation involves a necessary marginalisation of religious context. This is evident in secular settings where the traditional cosmological and disciplinary language that would usually accompany meditation is routinely dismissed and replaced with modern Western discourses. Many examples can be found in contemporary discussions of mindfulness meditation, where aspects of Buddhist cosmology—which includes gods, ghosts, demons and realms of rebirth—are reinterpreted in psychological, metaphoric, and symbolic terms. In *Mindful America*, Jeff Wilson (2014: 46–48) notes examples where, in popular mindfulness texts, the demon Mara is reduced to negative emotion, supernatural entities such as hungry ghosts are seen as metaphoric images for mental states such as desire and craving, and the metaphysical realms like the six realms of existence are re-imagined as "Six Patterns of Stress." The use of these metaphors is particularly common in applications of mindfulness to addiction recovery and mindful eating.

Buddhist cosmology is also reinterpreted in modernist versions of Tibetan Buddhism. In *The Myth of Freedom and the Way of Meditation*, Chogyam Trungpa (1976: 24), one of the most influential Tibetan Buddhist teachers in the modern West, describes the realms of rebirth in psychological terms:

> The realms are predominantly emotional attitudes towards ourselves and our surroundings—reinforced by conceptualisations and rationalisations. As human beings we may, during the course of a day, experience the emotions of all the realms, from the pride of the god realm to the hatred and paranoia of the hell realm. Nonetheless, a person's psychology is usually firmly rooted in one realm.

Maharishi Mahesh Yogi adopted a similar approach with TM when he translated Hindu concepts of gods into the language of science:

> The "gods" mentioned here are the deities presiding over the innumerable laws of nature, which are present everywhere throughout relative life. They are the powers governing different impulses of intelligence and energy, working out the evolution of everything in creation. The existence of gods may be understood by an analogy: each of the myriad cells in the human body has its own level of life, energy and intelligence; together, these innumerable lives produce human life. A human being is like a god to all these small impulses of energy and intelligence, each with its own form, tendencies, sphere of activity and influence, working for the purpose of evolution (Mahesh Yogi, 1989: 143–44).[28]

Some scholars have argued that meditation must be "sanitised" in this way in order to appeal to a secular Western audience. For example, in the case of mindfulness meditation, Jon Kabat-Zinn has argued that de-contextualisation is necessary in order to make meditation accessible to Westerners who would benefit from the practice but have no interest in Buddhism. Re-interpreting Buddhist ideas within a secular scientific framework helps to avoid associations with religion that would

---

[28] Humes (2010) argues that Mahesh also appropriated Hindu terms in new spellings so they did not appear to be religious. For example, "*siddhi*" became "sidhi" and "*yajna*" became "yagya."

undermine attempts to present mindfulness as an evidence-based and legitimate mainstream medical treatment. Regarding clinical mindfulness, Kabat-Zinn (2011: 282) writes: "I bent over backward to structure it and find ways to speak about it that avoided as much as possible the risk of it being seen as Buddhist, 'New Age,' 'Eastern Mysticism' or just plain 'flakey.'"

Simplification: psychological, pathological and neural reductionism

While the attempt to define meditation as scientific, or even as secular, has been met with scepticism from scientists and scholars of religion, meditation techniques have still been seen as objects worthy of scientific study. As discussed in previous chapters, there has been a large amount of scientific research conducted on the physiological and psychological outcomes of specific types of meditation, most commonly TM and mindfulness. As a result, researchers have sought pragmatic and simplified definitions of meditation that can be applied in research and clinical practice. So far, attempts to operationally define "meditation" have involved firstly, the removal of any religious associations, and secondly, the reduction of the term "meditation" to refer purely to suggested psychological or neurological mechanisms and processes. Reducing meditation to a biological or cognitive mechanism that is either non-religious (an inherent human capacity) or multi-religious (universal to all religions and therefore arguably more of a generic philosophy or worldview) makes it an acceptable secular object of study. This idea is illustrated in an early comment made by Herbert Benson, founder of the meditation "relaxation response," and colleagues (Kutz et al. 1985: 2):

> To understand the psychophysiological aspects of meditation, it should first be conceptually denuded of its cultural and religious biases. This is best achieved by defining meditation as an intentional regulation of attention from moment to moment, a definition that can be applied to all forms of meditation.

This early comment expresses a reductionist viewpoint that has, until perhaps very recently, permeated meditation research; that is, the idea that all meditation techniques can be reduced to an innate human capability (for example, attention regulation) and that religious context is simply an unnecessary add-on. Many similar examples of reductionism can be found throughout the psychological and clinical literature, where meditation has been variously re-conceptualised as a cognitive distraction technique, a self-regulation strategy, or a mental discipline aimed at training attention. In his book *Mindsight*, clinical professor of psychiatry Daniel Siegal writes: "People sometimes hear the word mindfulness and think 'religion.' But the reality is that focusing our attention in this way is a biological process that promotes health—a form of brain hygiene—not religion." Similarly, in *The Mindful Therapist*, Siegal argues that mindfulness is "a human skill that religions use—not itself a religious practice."[29] More recently science has turned towards neurological models, and within this paradigm meditative experiences have been explained in terms of concepts such as sensory deprivation, changes in the opioid systems, and by analogy to neural deficits such as amnesia, apraxia, or disordered spatial processing. Some scholars go so far as to recommend completely uncoupling "mindfulness" from the term "meditation" (Hayes and Shenk 2004).

While operational definitions are necessary for scientific studies and useful for practical applications, purely mechanistic interpretations of meditation that ignore context and reduce meditative phenomena to nothing but the suggested processes or mechanisms involved can result in inappropriate reductionism. Charles Tart (2008: 138) refers to this as *premature parsimony*:

> a common cognitive pathology in science where the desire to create a simple and elegant explanation for things results in ignoring important aspects of the actual phenomena. Although consciousness research has now become relatively respectable in contemporary psychology and neurology, the lure of premature parsimony is as strong as ever, and the field is rife with oversimplifications.

Reducing complex entities such as meditation to the sum of their constituent parts makes them easier to study. However, the cost of this reductionism is that the object that is being studied scientifically is no longer the object that appears naturally in the world. This is one of the shortfalls of scientific reductionism. In the case of meditation,

---

[29] These examples are taken from Wilson, *Mindful America*, 58.

trying to force all types of meditation and all meditative experiences into pre-existing Western categories may not be possible. This is particularly evident in the case of meditation-related altered states of consciousness. For example, Tart posits that various contemplative systems and practices have cognitions, emotions, and actions that are only fully accessible in appropriate altered states of consciousness; this is termed "state specific knowledge." State-specific knowledge is an embodied form of knowledge that can only be fully accessed in the appropriate altered state of consciousness. Hence, trying to explain meditation in scientific terms that are usually reserved for everyday "normal" states of consciousness, while still valuable, will inevitably overlook some of the important state-specific aspects of the experience.

Additionally, there has recently been a growing recognition of the important role of cultural context in meditative experience. Scholars such as Evan Thompson (2017) argue that meditation is a social practice; it involves the integration of a variety of cognitive, affective, and bodily skills *in situated action*. Hence, the cognitive functions involved in meditation practice cannot simply be reduced to particular brain areas or networks. This is because firstly, the correct level of description for any cognitive function is the embodied subject or person, not brain areas or networks, and secondly because it is unlikely that there is one-to-one mapping between particular cognitive functions and particular brain areas or neural networks, especially as currently identified by fMRI. Thompson notes that after examining large databases of neuroimaging data, the evidence suggests that there is no one-to-one correspondence between particular brain regions and particular cognition functions. Donald S. Lopez Jr. (2008: 209) also argues this point in *Buddhism and Science*, when he writes: "Even for *vipassana*, the 'mindfulness' practice widely studied by cognitive scientists, the goal is something far beyond anything easily measured on an fMRI." Other scholars note that meditative terms such as "enlightenment" are imprecise constructs that cannot be reduced to changes in neural correlates, cognition, or behaviour. For example, Davis and Vago (2013: 870) describe enlightenment as a "profound transformation across ethical, perceptual, emotional, and cognitive domains."

Similarly, in his article "The Myth of the Present Moment," Ronald Purser (2015) explores some limitations of Kabat-Zinn's present-moment focused operational definition of mindfulness. Purser argues that this definition is limited in that it does not consider systematic and structural causes of suffering. He posits that the central Buddhist goal of alleviating suffering, both for the self and for others, requires the meditator to go *beyond* concepts of the present moment to examine the nature of all aspects of conditioned existence—i.e. the broader world. Enhancing awareness in the present moment is not an end in itself; it is merely a means to provide the necessary conditions for engaging with the broader world. This engagement also involves a moral and ethical component which arguably cannot be separated from mindfulness practice (e.g. Stanley et al. 2018).

Re-contextualisation: "the buddha was a scientist" and the creation of a western meditation lineage

Another key way that meditation has been detached from religion is through the presentation of meditation as a technique that is compatible with modern Western scientific values. This is usually achieved by emphasising the psychological and philosophical components of Eastern religions as opposed to elements such as ritual or doctrine. Specifically, Buddhist and Hindu scriptures often contain detailed psychological theories that attempt to describe and explain human experience and behaviour. These theories cover aspects of psychology such as cognition, behaviour, emotion, and personality, and contemporary Western advocates of meditation tend to draw comparisons between these religious systems and modern Western theories of philosophy and psychology (Sedlmeier and Srinivas 2016). Popular modern interpretations of Buddhism for example, tend to present the historical Buddha as someone who taught a philosophy, or a way of life, not a religion. This viewpoint is reflected in comments made by early Orientalists and Buddhist sympathisers such as Paul Carus (1852–1919) and Harold Fielding-Hall (1859–1917), who described the Buddha as the "first prophet of the Religion of Science"[30] and the "Newton of the spiritual world."[31]

The view of the Buddha as a scientist-philosopher, and of Buddhism as a type of science, is still quite prevalent today and is one of the characteristic features of Buddhist modernism. It is also a view that is held in the Western *vipassana* community, particularly in the Goenka lineage. Contemporary *vipassana* pioneer S.N. Goenka (2002) referred to

---

[30] Cited in McMahan, *The Making*, 109.
[31] Cited in Lopez, *Buddhism and Science*, 154.

the original Buddha as a "super-scientist" who discovered truths about the mind that are only now being revealed by contemporary Western science. Similarly, when discussing the historical Buddhist origins of mindfulness meditation, Jon Kabat-Zinn (2003: 145) writes:

> One might think of the historical Buddha as, among other things, a born scientist and physician who had nothing in the way of instrumentation other than his own mind and body and experience, yet managed to use these native resources to great effect to delve into the nature of suffering and the human condition. What emerged from this arduous and single-minded contemplative investigation was a series of profound insights, a comprehensive view of human nature, and a formal "medicine" for treating its fundamental "dis-ease" ...

The re-imagining of the Buddha as a scientist naturally re-conceptualises meditation as a mode of scientific enquiry; if the Buddha was a scientist, then Buddhism is a science, and meditation is a secular tool for scientific exploration. Along these lines S.N. Goenka often referred to *vipassana* meditation as a scientific method of investigating consciousness. Similarly, the influential German-born monk Nyanaponika Thera (1901–1994), who was highly influential in the development and popularisation of mindfulness in the West prior to the 1970s, described Buddhist meditation as a "science of the mind" and equated the bare attention component of mindfulness meditation with the scientific mindset (McMahan 2008: 206). This view is still very popular with quite a few scholars, although it is perhaps retreating as recent meditation research emphasises the critical role of context and social cognition.

Examples of scientific re-contextualisation are also found in TM, which was presented by Maharishi Mahesh Yogi as a secular technique that was compatible with science. However, scholar Cynthia Humes (2010: 349) notes that TM had less-than-secular beginnings; in 1959 Mahesh founded the Spiritual Regeneration Movement in the United States, an organisation whose articles of incorporation explicitly state "this corporation is a religious one." Humes argues that after several years of "limited response to his evangelism in the West," Mahesh began claiming that his teachings did not require a belief in God, were not specifically Hindu, and not actually religious at all. Rather Mahesh promoted the TM practice as a "natural" technique that transcended religious dogma and which was part of an essentialist philosophy that he referred to as the "Science of Creative Intelligence." Modern advocates of Hindu and Buddhist-derived forms of meditation often posit that, like science, these traditions are pointing towards some ultimate perennial truth or reality. For example, D.T. Suzuki presented Zen meditation as a way of realising a universal reality to which all religions, and some secular philosophies, aspire. Similarly, when discussing mindfulness meditation, Kabat-Zinn (2003: 145) writes: "Of course, the Buddha himself was not a Buddhist. One might think of dharma as a sort of universal generative grammar, an innate set of empirically testable rules" and hence, mindfulness, "being about attention, is also of necessity universal. There is nothing particularly Buddhist about it."

While Mahesh's philosophy placed less emphasis on meditation as a technique for systematically studying the mind, it did attempt to give scientific legitimacy to TM via the establishment of universities, journals, and quasi-academic conferences (Humes 2010). Mahesh also employed other approaches such as re-describing traditional Advaita Vedanta philosophy and practices in more neutral Western language, using metaphors and analogies based in Western scientific concepts, and claiming parallels between ancient Vedic teachings and the modern sciences of quantum physics and biochemistry. (For a critique of this type of parallelism between science and mysticism see Jones 2010.)

A final mode of re-contextualisation worth considering is the creation of a modern Western secular meditation lineage via the transference of authority from monks to laypeople. In *Mindful America*, Jeff Wilson (2014) notes that in contemporary Western discussions of meditation, the dialogue is now clearly dominated by lay voices. In the 1960s and 1970s, popular Western meditation teachers such as Joseph Goldstein, Jack Kornfield, and Sharon Salzberg were instructed by ordained monks in Asia. However, today the majority of meditation teachers being trained are laypeople who may have never travelled to Asia, visited a monastery, or attended a retreat. In the case of mindfulness meditation, Wilson (2014: 50) writes:

> A second generation of lay teachers swiftly began to emerge who had mainly or only practiced Buddhism in America, had personal exposure to only limited selections of Buddhist tradition, and were taught either by a mixture of missionary monks and lay Americans, or only by other Americans.

In *Luminous Passage*, Charles Prebish (1999: 152) argues that to a large extent American *vipassana* teachers presented meditation in a context almost wholly removed from association with the Theravada tradition. For example, Kornfield is quoted in a 1995 interview as saying: "We wanted to offer the powerful practices of insight meditation, as many of our teachers did, as simply as possible without the complications of rituals, robes, chanting and the whole religious tradition." As a result, the Buddhist-derived practice of mindfulness has now lost much of its connection to renunciation; there has been a diminishment of the retreat model, and lay teaching and lay practice have been normalised. Further, in an age where it is no longer even necessary to have a meditation teacher—since meditation can be learned from books, blogs, internet forums, apps, and online courses—monastic institutions may be viewed as unnecessary, conservative, and inconvenient. Lay life is increasingly viewed as the best place to practise meditation and the emphasis is shifting towards pragmatic and efficient techniques that can be practised during daily life and "off the cushion."

CHAPTER FIVE

Meditation divorced from religion

> *The least recognised time bomb of the 20th century may be contact between the Asian meditation traditions and Western culture. At their best, these traditions offer a portal into a radically new (lived) understanding of what it is to know, to be, to act, and to be an embodied self in time. Western approaches have so far tended only to nibble around the edges of these traditions.*
>
> —Eleanor Rosch.[32]

Meditation adverse effects in religious traditions

In the contemporary West, the proponents of meditation techniques such as TM, mindfulness and *vipassana* have, at times, gone to great lengths to distance themselves from religion and present their techniques as rational and secular. However, this disconnection from traditional meditation teachers, monastic environments, and texts may be a key factor that has contributed to meditation adverse effects being overlooked. In Eastern religions, traditional commentaries, stages-of-the-path literature, and biographical narratives acknowledge

---

[32] E. Rosch, "Is Wisdom in the Brain?," *Psychological Science* 10, no.3 (1999): 222.

difficulties associated with meditation practice. For example, Eric Greene (2017: 373) writes that Buddhist meditation has traditionally been seen as both a high risk and high reward practice:

> Given its frequent presentation in the modern West as a panacea for psychological or even physical ailments, it might be surprising to find that Buddhist meditation has often been seen as potentially dangerous. The otherwise highly praised Buddhist meditations on the impurity of the body can, according to a famous canonical story, lead to suicide; elsewhere we learn that meditation on the breath—a common introductory meditation practice—can, if performed improperly, disturb the body's "winds" and lead to death. The Buddha himself is said to have been attacked by demons—in the form of the hosts of Mara—on the eve of his awakening, precisely on account of his advanced levels of meditative attainment.

In Theravada Buddhism, adverse effects associated with meditation are well-known and may be due to the *dukkha nanas* (Pali: insights into suffering), a series of insights that are characterised by fear, misery, and disgust and which can cause mental distress. These experiences are well-documented in Buddhist manuals such as the *Visuddhimagga* (The Path of Purification), the *Vimuttimaga* (The Path of Freedom), and the *Abhidhamma*, and are usually interpreted as milestones on the path to enlightenment. Lois VanderKooi (1997: 32–33) provides a concise description of the *dukkha nanas*:

> As outlined in the *Visuddhimagga* (a fifth-century work that supposedly collects the Buddha's teachings on meditative states), the process of realising *nirvana* is fraught with troubling and sometimes excruciating states. Initially, confusion, hallucinations, disturbing feelings, and involuntary movements can occur as one gains knowledge of mental and physical states through increasing concentration and mindfulness. As *samadhi* is achieved, "pseudo-*nirvana*" experiences of rapture, tranquillity, and bliss can be accompanied by frightening images, uncomfortable body sensations such as itching, heat, and stiffness, and gastrointestinal problems of nausea, vomiting, and diarrhea. Then, sadness, irritability, extreme fear, and a deep sense of the insipid nature of life may manifest

as one becomes more and more aware of the arising and passing away of phenomena. A desire for deliverance can emerge, and one may wish to discontinue practice. For example, the body may itch as though being bitten by ants. Later, when deciding to practice to completion, one may feel odd sensations such as being slashed by a knife.

The *samatha-vipassana* meditation manual, written by Sramaṇa Zhiyi (538–597 CE), founder of the Tiantai tradition of Buddhism in China, has a chapter dedicated to the diagnosis and treatment of meditation-related disorders. According to this text, meditation-related pathology may develop as a result of imbalance during practice:

> Once the practitioner has established his resolve to cultivating the Path, disorders associated with the four great elements may manifest. Based on one's present application of the contemplative mind, the breath may be caused to provoke the activation of latent disorders. Sometimes it happens that one is unable to skilfully and appropriately adjust the three factors of body, mind and breath. Due to interferences between the inward and outward circumstances, pathological trouble may develop … if one is able to skilfully apply the mind, then the four hundred and four kinds of disorders will naturally be cured. If, however, one fails in the correct placement of the mind, then the four hundred and four kinds of disorders may arise on that very account (Dharmamitra 2009: 169).

Adverse effects associated with meditation are also documented in Zen Buddhism. For example, there is a category of meditative experiences that may arise during *zazen* practice, called *makyo* (translated as "diabolic phenomenon," from *ma* [devil] and *kyo* [phenomenon; objective world]). Hence, *makyo* are disturbing phenomena, and can include visual, auditory, and olfactory hallucinations, and involuntary movements. In *The Three Pillars of Zen*, American Zen teacher Roshi Philip Kapleau notes that the number of *makyo* which can appear to a meditator are unlimited; in the Ryogon sutra the Buddha warns of fifty different kinds of *makyo*, but these are just the most common manifestations, and experiences may vary according to the personality and temperament of the individual meditator. Kapleau (2000: 45) writes: "While disciplining himself in meditation the Yogin is liable to be visited by all kinds of evil beings whereby he is constantly assailed by hallucinations of various natures. These are all due to highly accentuated nervous derangements, and the Yogin is advised to guard himself against them."

Zen traditions also acknowledge a prolonged illness-like condition related to meditation, called "Zen sickness" or "meditation sickness." This condition is understood to manifest due to a variety of causes that may be physiological, psychological, karmic, or supernatural in nature. Depending on the cause, Zen sickness may manifest in different ways (for example, as headaches, tightness in the chest or fearful hallucinations), and traditional teachers recommend an assortment of treatments ranging from modern medical and psychological care to traditional mantras, spells and repentance practices (Nelson 2012).

In Tibetan Buddhism, *nyams* (meditation experiences) may include adverse effects such as intense body pain, physiological disorders, paranoia, sadness, anger and fear. Additionally, there is a specific meditation-related condition that the Tibetans call *lung* (Epstein and L. Rapgay: 1989). In Tibetan medicine, *lung* (or *rlung*) is sometimes literally translated as "wind" or "wind illness," and unbalanced or disordered flows of *lung* are a key way in which psychiatric disorders are explained. Sometimes described as a nervous disorder or "meditator's disease," there are several different types of *lung* that are said to result from the interaction between meditation practice and characteristics of the individual meditator, such as imbalances in the meditator's constitution or their *karma*. Interestingly, Tibetan theories of *lung* seem to correspond with Western concepts of the autonomic nervous system (Samuel 2019).

In *Balanced Mind, Balanced Body*, Amy Cayton (2016) describes various treatments for *lung*, which come from both Tibetan folklore and more experienced meditators from the lay community. These include *bodhichitta* and *tonglen* practice, prostrations, mantras, traditional Tibetan medicine, and changes to diet and sleep. Cayton notes that meditators are advised to consult a qualified teacher or Tibetan doctor to treat *lung* and that without treatment it can become a chronic state that is difficult to deal with. Cayton (2016: 48) writes:

> When we talk about *lung*, we must distinguish between acute and chronic *lung*. In this essay, I'm mainly concerned with acute *lung*, specifically that which arises in meditation retreats. Acute *lung* can come from concentrating too hard on the mandala, reciting mantras

too fast, working too hard in service or at our jobs, or frustration in relationships. With rest and Tibetan medicine (if we can get it), this form of *lung* goes away when we finish our retreat or stop doing what was causing our mental stress. Chronic *lung*, or *tsok lung*, is what we might label as varying degrees of post-traumatic stress disorder (PTSD). Chronic *lung* can be treated with herbs, diet, acupuncture, Tibetan medicine, and verbal therapies.

Hindu and Yogic traditions also acknowledge periods of difficulty associated with meditation practice, most often associated with *kundalini*, which is said to be the biological mechanism behind enlightenment (Greyson 1993). Classical esoteric literature describes kundalini as a normally dormant force that resides at the base of the spine, and that when awakened, can cause a variety of mental, emotional, physical and spiritual effects. According to some modern accounts, kundalini should only be awakened as a gradual process, under the guidance of an experienced teacher. If a kundalini awakening occurs when a meditator is not properly prepared, it can cause negative effects, including fear, disorientation, and psychosis—a "kundalini crisis" (Sannella 1989). The most well-known descriptions of kundalini crisis are modern biographical accounts, such as that of Gopi Krishna (1903–1984), an Indian yogi and mystic who wrote about his own long-lasting kundalini crisis which included symptoms of depression, insomnia, and psychosis-like states (Krishna 2001). More recently, there have been modern case reports that describe mental health problems attributed to kundalini (Valanciute and Thampy 2011). In *The Healing Gods*, Gunther Brown (2013: 133) cites examples of kundalini problems related to hatha yoga and pranayama:

> Although many instructors tout yoga's safety, some yoga proponents warn of physical, psychological, and spiritual risks. Swami Swatmarama, of Yoga Vidya Gurukul University, cautions that performing pranayama in hatha yoga awakens kundalini energy rapidly: "But if one is not prepared to take on this high level energy awakening then this may have negative effects on mind and body." Swami Narayanananda is more specific about what negative effects might entail: "if a person does not know how to check the currents and to bring down the partly risen kundalini shakti to safer centers, one suffers terribly and it may ruin the whole life of a person or lead one to insanity."

However, it is not clear that problems with kundalini were ever mentioned in classical texts. Some scholars have argued that because the ancient traditions provided gurus to supervise kundalini awakenings, the classical literature did not focus on problems associated with the phenomena; it was assumed that with proper context and proper guidance, the process would lead to positive outcomes (Greyson 1993).

In sum, meditation adverse effects are mentioned across a variety of religious traditions. The literature observes that meditation adverse effects may arise simply as a normal stage on the path of progress towards enlightenment (for example, *makyo* and the *dukkha nanas*), or if the practice is not undertaken with adequate preparation, in the right conditions, and with proper guidance (such as is the case with Zen sickness, *lung* and kundalini crisis). However, when secular meditation is disconnected from these traditional religious sources, this knowledge regarding adverse effects is often lost. The next section will examine four domains of meditation practice and discuss how adverse effects are recognised and managed within each of these domains in traditional contexts, and how they are often overlooked in secular contexts.

Preparation

Something all the major meditative traditions have in common is a belief in rigorous preparation; that is, in order to safely achieve the desired states and outcomes of meditation, an individual must adequately prepare before undertaking any actual meditation practice. For example, in the Hindu-derived discipline of *yoga*, preparatory methods consist of several stages and many steps, including moral and religious training (*yama* and *niyama*), posture practice (*asana*), breath control (*pranayama*), diet changes and behavioural modifications. These preliminary practices are then followed by sense withdrawal practices (*pratyahara*) and concentration techniques (*dharana*) which finally prepare the individual for meditation (*dhyana*) and meditative absorption (*samadhi*). In *Yogic Meditation*, Georg Feuerstein (2006) describes how for meditation to be successful, certain prerequisites must be met, including correct posture (sitting erect with the spine and neck aligned, *riju-kaya*), a suitable environment, the development of concentration and self-discipline, and the cultivation of nonattachment (*vairagya*), which depends on emotional and spiritual maturity. In the yogic traditions, practice must begin with this preliminary training, otherwise progress is not possible. Feuerstein (2006: 105) notes:

> Without adequate moral preparation and genuine spiritual aspiration, meditation tends to be experienced as routine, tedious, or impossible. Hence Patanjali's eightfold path begins with the five moral observances (*yama*) of nonharming (*ahimsa*), truthfulness (*satya*), nonstealing (*asteya*), chastity (*brahmacarya*), and greedlessness (*aparigraha*). A second foundation is *niyama*, self-discipline, which Patanjali divides into the five practices of purity (*shauca*), contentment (*samtosha*), austerity (*tapas*), study (*svadhyaya*), and dedication to a higher principle, specifically the "Lord" (*ishvara-pranidhana*).

Similarly, in Buddhism, meditation is seen as an advanced practice that is only started once an individual has mastered preliminary instruction and discipline. In Theravada Buddhism, meditation practice has three components—morality (*sila*), concentration or calm abiding (*samatha*), and insight (*vipassana*)—which correspond to the Eightfold Path. Practice begins with morality, as it is believed that the mind must be purified of "unwholesome" or unvirtuous thoughts in order to facilitate initial concentration. For lay practitioners, five moral precepts are taken before beginning meditation practice: abstaining from killing, stealing, lying, sexual misconduct, and intoxicants. For novice meditators the list of precepts increases to ten, and for monks there are more than 300 prohibitions and observances that regulate every detail of monastic life (Hickey 2008). Once the meditator has attained a purified mind, the next step is to develop concentration or one-pointedness by fixing the mind on a single object; the meditation subject. The ability to concentrate then assists the meditator in the pursuit of insight. Thus, the interaction between morality, concentration and insight cannot be separated; morality facilitates initial concentration, which then enables sustained insight. A similar process operates in Zen Buddhism and Tibetan Buddhism.

In religious contexts, morality and concentration training is the foundation of meditation practice and is seen to be a necessary requirement for the development of insight. This is generally thought to be because one cannot have peace of mind, and hence a stable mind, if one's behaviour is unethical. For example, Andrea Grabovac and colleagues (2011) argue that from a modern psychological perspective, one of the major purposes of ethics in meditation is to reduce the baseline amount of mental proliferation that an individual might experience. By leading an ethical life, a meditator should naturally experience reduced negative affect (such as guilt, doubts, and worries), which in turn supports both concentration and mindfulness practices. Other scholars have argued that meditation without ethics can be dissatisfying and frustrating, leading only to superficial calmness but no lasting positive change, and that the inclusion of ethics in secular meditation practices may actually speed up progress and make insights more widely generalisable. While there is debate surrounding the extent to which ethics currently is or is not included in secular mindfulness practices, most modern Western adaptations of meditation skip these preparatory stages. Both mindfulness meditation and *vipassana* are focused primarily on insight practice and do not offer specific preparatory training in concentration or ethics.

Teaching meditation without adequate preparation can lead to problems. For example, in *Psychotherapy Without the Self*, Mark Epstein (2007: 14) describes a "disturbing trend" noted by Western psychotherapists when observing Western meditators:

> Western students of Eastern spiritual traditions who jumped into intensive meditation with little preparation sometimes experienced emotional distress. Many sincere practitioners, disillusioned with therapy or with the idea of therapy, turned to meditation in the hope of healing psychological issues and found that emotional material was uncovered that neither they nor their meditation teachers were prepared to deal with.

Contemporary Buddhist meditation teacher Culadasa (John Yates) argues that psychological problems arise when insight meditation is practised without the cultivation of advanced skill in concentration (*samatha*) or the experience of meditative absorption (*jhana*). As mentioned above, the modern *vipassana* tradition is a "dry insight" (non-*jhanic*) tradition and teaches that insight can be achieved without training in concentration; thus *samatha* and *jhana* are rarely mentioned, let alone taught, in this popular form of meditation. Culadasa argues that dry insight practices can lead to adverse effects, as *samatha* makes it easier for meditators to confront potentially de-stabilising insights into impermanence, emptiness, suffering and non-self. The joy, tranquillity and equanimity of *samatha* provide an important "lubricating" quality or palliative that relieves the internal friction associated with challenging insights. He writes:

> Without *samatha*, these challenging Insights have the potential to send a practitioner spiralling into a "dark night of the soul." This Christian term comes originally from the writings of St. John of the Cross, who supposedly spent forty-five years in this dark night. The term beautifully captures the feelings of despair, meaninglessness, non-specific anxiety, frustration, and anger that often accompany such powerful realisations (Culadasa 2015: 412).

In both clinical mindfulness-based interventions and *vipassana*, preparation in concentration is not seen as a necessary prerequisite to begin meditation; hence, teachers of these techniques are unlikely to attribute any adverse effects that might show up to an "unbalanced" insight meditation practice.[33] If meditation adverse effects do occur, they may instead be explained as simply being due to "psychological issues." For example, *vipassana* meditation retreats are generally promoted as suitable for anyone in reasonable physical and mental health. These retreats do not require any preparation, despite the fact that a *vipassana* retreat involves ten days of seated silent meditation—a physical and mental challenge for most novice meditators. Indeed, in an article titled "Is Mindfulness Safe?" published on the Oxford Mindfulness Centre website, Baer and Kuyken (2016) note that the most intensive way to practise mindfulness is on meditation retreats and "most reports of adverse effects of mindfulness practice to date come from participants in intensive retreats." They also report that "Anecdotal evidence suggests that harm is rare, but a few participants have reported severe psychological problems lasting for months or years after the retreat has ended."

---

[33] Referring back to the early Zen, Dzogchen and Theravada reformers, Sharf (2015: 476) notes that all these traditions have been criticised for "dumbing down" the Buddhist tradition by devaluing ethical training and the role of concentration. Also, it is worth noting that too much concentration meditation at the expense of insight meditation has also been said to lead to adverse effects, particularly the re-experiencing of trauma, e.g. L. Brasington, "Leigh Brasington Interview" https://vimeo.com/61893225. Accessed September 2018.

Supportive context

In religious traditions, meditation practices have corresponding psychologies, philosophies, and belief systems that work to conceptualise and frame their insights. Traditional texts and cosmologies provide a cartography and context for clarifying different types of meditation experience. In contemporary Western applications of meditation, most or all of the religious context for meditation practices is reinterpreted, minimised, or left out, and research findings on meditation are interpreted almost exclusively within Western psychological frameworks. However, due to cultural and conceptual differences, Western secular frameworks may not be able to provide an appropriate context within which meditators can understand their experiences and frame their insights. In particular, Buddhist insights into emptiness, impermanence, non-self and suffering tend to contradict the current Western operating model of reality. That is, the dominant Western paradigm for understanding "reality" assumes that objects exist, that an independent, autonomous self exists, and that positive or negative experiences result from the interaction between the two. These beliefs provide the foundation for a sense of meaning and purpose in life, and meditation-induced insights that challenge or conflict with these assumptions can be severely disruptive, leading to adverse effects such as anxiety and despair.

Other cultural and conceptual differences relate to states of consciousness. Western culture is predominantly monophasic; that is, almost exclusively focused on the ordinary waking state of consciousness, with perceptual and cognitive processes oriented toward the external world. Traditional meditative cultures, however, tend to be polyphasic; that is, they place importance on other functional but non-ordinary states of consciousness that may be the result of dreams, trance states, meditation states, or intoxicants (Walsh and Shapiro 2006). In religious traditions, meditation is often used to achieve altered states of consciousness (ASC), which are defined as experiences that produce "a qualitative alteration in the overall pattern of mental functioning, such that the experiencer feels his consciousness is radically different from the way it functions ordinarily" (Tart 1972). In particular, meditative disciplines value and cultivate altered states where one's sense of identity extends beyond the individual self. Scholars of religion note that meditation-related ASCs are considered both attainable and important, and there is a vast literature on these experiences from many, if not all, the major traditions. In religious contexts ASCs allow the individual to access state-specific knowledge that may be used to heal or to serve their community, and people who experience meditation-related ASCs have reported profound and lasting positive changes in their lives, including radical shifts in their values and belief systems. While ASCs are not the end goal of meditation practice, they appear to change the cognitive and behavioural patterns of the meditator, thereby enhancing wellbeing and quality of life.

Modern meditation studies suggest that secular forms of meditation can lead to spiritual and mystical experiences, including ASCs (e.g. Kornfield 1979). While Western psychologists may have rediscovered some of these states (for example, Maslow's "peak experiences," Jung's "numinous" experience, Grof's "holotropic" experience, Fromm's "atonement" and James' "cosmic consciousness"), without a conceptual framework through which to understand them, these states may be experienced negatively. In particular, in modern Western settings, altered states may be mis-categorised as psychosis, dissociation, or depersonalisation, leading to what transpersonal psychologists have termed a "spiritual emergency." Spiritual emergency is defined as significant distress associated with spiritual practices and experiences that causes a disruption to psychological, social, and occupational functioning. Stanislav and Christina Grof (1989) are credited with coining the term (also known as "spiritual emergence") in the 1960s in order to define a range of psychological difficulties that Westerners were encountering when engaging in Eastern spiritual practices. They argue that one of the most important causes of spiritual emergency is deep involvement in various forms of meditation and spiritual practice.

Psychologist David Lukoff notes that individuals in the midst of a spiritual emergency may appear to have a mental illness if viewed out of context, but they are actually undergoing a normal reaction to spiritual development that is non-pathological and distinct from psychopathology (e.g. Lukoff et al. 1998). Those who believe in the concept of spiritual emergency argue that the symptoms of spiritual emergency may appear similar to, and sometimes identical with, psychopathology, however their causes and significance are very different, and hence treatment should be different (Bronn and McIlwain 2015).

There is some recognition of spiritual emergency in modern clinical psychology. For example, the Diagnostic and Statistical Manual,

Fifth Edition (DSM-V) acknowledges some distressing religious and spiritual issues as non-pathological by including a category entitled "Religious or Spiritual Problem" (V62.89). Introducing V-code 62.89 has increased the possibility of differential diagnosis between religious/spiritual problems and psychopathology. The DSM-V also recognises the need to distinguish between psychopathology and meditation-related experiences in instances of depersonalisation and derealisation:

> Volitionally induced experiences of depersonalisation/derealisation can be a part of meditative practices that are prevalent in many religions and cultures and should not be diagnosed as a disorder. However, there are individuals who initially induce these states intentionally but over time lose control over them and may develop a fear and aversion for related practices (DSM-V 2013: 304).

However, despite numerous psychologists, academics, and medical professionals attesting to the existence of these problems, spiritual issues have been largely neglected in mainstream psychology and Western health professionals report minimal or no training in dealing with them. This could be for a number of reasons, including bias against religion and spirituality in the field of psychology (for example, research indicates psychologists tend to be much less religious than their clients), and a lack of commonly agreed upon guidelines. The inclusion of spirituality and religion in the treatment of people with severe mental illness has also been seen as problematic due to the possibility that spiritual and religious ideation may worsen symptoms of disorganisation, trigger harm to self or others, or promote lack of adherence to treatment recommendations (Fallot 2001). An emphasis on establishing psychology as a scientific discipline may have also led to a reluctance to acknowledge the relevance of spirituality and religion resulting in what some scholars have termed "spiritually avoidant care" (Vieten et al. 2013). Lack of training in religious and spiritual diversity may have significant consequences for clinical practice, as not only may meditation-related adverse effects be misdiagnosed as psychopathology, but there is evidence to suggest that psychologists can hold explicit and implicit negative biases based on perceived client religiosity, such as assessing religious clients as having worse prognoses (Vieten et al. 2016). However, the increasing popularity of mindfulness-based therapeutic interventions and growing recognition of the diversity of meditation-related phenomenology (both positive and negative) may indicate an imminent paradigm shift in the way that spiritual and religious issues are approached in health settings (Sperry 2012).

Teacher and technique

In traditional religious contexts the ideal meditation training is one-to-one transmission from teacher to student, with practice generally undertaken in isolation.[34] In Buddhism, the ideal meditation teacher was the historical Buddha, who was said to know the mind and heart of others, and could therefore perfectly match an individual with their appropriate meditation object and setting. In lieu of such a perfect teacher, the *Visuddhimagga* recommends that a meditation teacher should be selected according to their own level of attainment in meditation, with the most highly accomplished meditators being the most qualified teachers. The teacher's support and guidance is seen as critical, particularly when dealing with issues of technique, altered states of consciousness and the integration of insight.

In religious traditions, one of the fundamental roles of a meditation teacher is to give precise instruction regarding correct meditation technique, as incorrect technique can lead to adverse effects. Physical problems may result from improper posture (for example, neck and back pain), unnatural breathing (for example, a stressed diaphragm), or from lack of attendance to the physical environment (for example, inadequate clothing, food and sleep) (Nelson 2012: 66). Additionally, many meditative traditions note that adverse effects may occur as the result of an imbalanced practice; that is, excessive and over-vigorous meditation practice at the expense of other activities such as the study of scriptures or physical work. For example, the Zen teacher D.T. Suzuki emphasised the need for meditators to engage in physical activity in order to counterbalance sitting meditation. This may account for the inclusion of physical work practices (for example, gardening) and walking meditation (*kinhin*, which is alternated with periods of *zazen*) in Western Zen Centres (Nelson 2012: 75–78). Excessive seated meditation practice may

---

[34] In *Re-Enchantment*, Jeffery Paine (2004), writes that when Tibetan lamas saw people meditating in groups at American Zen centres, they saw this as being unusual, because in Tibet, meditation was a solitary activity.

lead to physical problems, as described by Dutch author Janwillem van de Wetering in *Afterzen*:

> Prolonged *zazen* gave me chronic hemorrhoids. Baba told me the human body is not designed to sit in the double or even the half lotus position for long periods of time. The postures put excessive strain on the rectum. I found that easy to believe. Preparation H is a staple in Zen monasteries, together with Maalox, for eating too hot meals too fast, peer pressure by zealots, too little sleep, and the relentless master's constant urging to solve a *koan* create mental tensions that ulcerate Zen stomachs (van de Wetering 1999: 4).

Psychological adverse effects may also result from excessive practice. For example, in Tibetan Buddhism, forcing the mind to stay on the meditation object in an overly rigid way is said to induce a psychiatric condition that is similar to an obsessive anxiety state (Epstein 2007: 149). Similarly, in Zen, overly rigorous practice and excessive striving for enlightenment, especially at the expense of engagement with the scriptures, is said to lead to a state described in the literature as "falling into emptiness" (*duokong*), which is associated with "meditation sickness" (*chanbing*). In this state, the meditator:

> loses touch with the socially, culturally, and historically constructed world in which he or she lives. The practitioner becomes estranged from the web of social relations that are the touchstone of our humanity as well as our sanity (Sharf 2015: 476).

Contemporary Buddhist teachers have argued that adverse effects such as *duokong* and *chanbing* result from a misinterpretation of the insight into emptiness (*śūnyatā*). The traditional Buddhist meaning of emptiness is that phenomena have no inherent nature by themselves, however in modern meditative contexts emptiness is sometimes misunderstood as a type of nihilism, leading to feelings of depression, anxiety and dissociation. Regarding emptiness, Richmond writes:

> If we can't understand such a profound concept, we often "lazily" associate Emptiness with Nihilism. The problem begins with the English translation of the original Sanskrit term *Shunyata*. This profound and complex concept is often translated into English as

"voidness." Voidness sounds a lot like "nothingness" and, in my many years of attending teachings, I've often heard teachers interchange the word Emptiness, Voidness and Nothingness, so this can be confusing from the get-go. In the same discussion, some teachers will warn against nihilism, but never-the-less use the word "nothingness."[35]

Contemporary Buddhist teacher Shinzen Young (2009), claims that difficulty integrating insights into emptiness and non-self (*anatta*) can actually result in adverse psychological effects that present as identical to depersonalisation and derealisation disorders (DP/DR). Young describes this phenomenon as an enlightenment experience gone wrong, or "enlightenment's evil twin." Ordinarily, an insight into emptiness and non-self is experienced as a fulfilling and empowering event, however, in some people, this insight is experienced as a nihilistic dysfunctional state. Young stresses that when insights are experienced as negative rather than empowering, this indicates that the meditator requires intervention and support from a senior competent teacher who knows how to deal with this issue successfully. Similarly, in *Zen Wisdom*, Buddhist teacher Master Sheng-yen (1931–2009) writes:

> If the teacher is not around and the person has an experience of emptiness, but not necessarily enlightenment, he or she could develop mental problems or become deeply confused. That is why practice traditions such as Chan, Zen, and Tibetan Buddhism stress the need for a qualified teacher.[36]

This view is also supported by findings from Sean Pritchard's (2016) qualitative study of *vipassana* meditators. Pritchard found that skilful guidance and conceptualisation by a teacher allowed students to successfully frame difficult meditation insights both in practice and within daily life. In particular, he cites an example of a student experiencing an

---

[35] L. Richmond, "What the Teachers Say About Emptiness: Removing 'Lazy Nihilism' from Shunyata—or 'How Deep the Rabbit Hole Goes' and 'How Big is the Moon?'" *Buddha Weekly*, https://buddhaweekly.com/what-the-teachers-say-about-emptiness-removing-lazy-nihilism-from-shunyata-or-how-deep-the-rabbit-hole-goes-and-how-big-is-the-moon/. Accessed December 2019.
[36] Cited in Nelson, "Chan (Zen) Sickness," 91.

extreme case of the *dukkha nanas*, which was then put into an appropriate context by the teacher:

> I actually became suicidal and I was afraid to tell V. [teacher], that he'd never allow me to come back. I was in the *dukkha-nanas*. I was in the misery, and I thought, I never had this. And then I went and I saw V. when it was time for me to go for the interview. And he said this is common in this particular time and that other yogis had gone through it too ... Then once I got to V., I think just being with him and him kind of making light of it, it was, like, this is just the practice. He gave me a context of that and, like, this is good. The stronger it is the better. "This is good fear. Go back and practice." For some reason it really worked (Pritchard 2016: 73).

Pritchard argues that practical, technical advice and clear specific instructions from a qualified teacher can prevent extreme negative mental states from lasting, whereas when unguided, meditators might become stuck in states of fear, anxiety, terror, depression, or psychosis for extended periods that could last from days to years.

Experienced meditation teachers are also able to recognise, and provide guidance and contextualisation regarding, altered states of consciousness. In a qualitative study, Lois VanderKooi interviewed twelve Buddhist teachers (four Zen, four Theravadan, four Tibetan, all teaching in North America) regarding their experiences with extreme mental states in Western meditation students. All of the teachers understood altered states of consciousness (including disturbing emotions and fantasies, perceptual anomalies and hallucinations, memories, proprioceptive sensations and movements, and psychotic-like experiences) as phenomena that often emerge in early stages of Buddhist meditation and as meditation practice progresses. For example, Theravada teachers estimated that during a three-month long retreat about half of the students experience altered states.

VanderKooi notes that all the teachers had various strategies for effectively dealing with these altered states, and as a result they did not often encounter extreme adverse effects. The teachers' strategies included providing assurance that the experience is normal and will pass, adjusting the meditation technique, checking for correct posture and breathing, decreasing meditation time, adding "grounding" physical activities, conducting more frequent interviews with the student, and recommending changes to diet. The teachers were also able to identify warning signs that an extreme altered state may lead to a psychotic break, and knew when meditation practice should be discontinued and medical advice sought. One Tibetan teacher noted that advanced meditators need a qualified teacher to help differentiate between psychotic states and true spiritual visions.

Similarly, Buddhist teacher Alan Wallace (2011: 146) describes how an experienced teacher can provide a metaphorical map for their student's meditation practice:

> the mind ... is very delicate. If you are meditating on your own, making it up as you go, you might be lucky. But if you do any type of meditative practice intensively, it's like setting out on a ship. If you're just one degree off, you can wind up hundreds of miles away from where you intended to go. Over the last thirty-five years ... I've encountered a number of people who have run into very deep psychological problems, including psychosis. Usually it occurred when they were not practicing under the guidance of a skillful, knowledgeable, and compassionate teacher. An open and trusting relationship with a teacher is a great safety net.

In secular mindfulness meditation settings, the importance of the role of the teacher in identifying and dealing with adverse effects is acknowledged. For example, the Melbourne Academic Mindfulness Interest Group states that short-term adverse experiences can be a transient part of the MBI process, and "the skill of the instructor in dealing with such eventualities may be important in determining whether they become valuable learning opportunities or, alternatively, adverse events" (Dobkin et al. 2012: 47). Burrows (2017: 39) also argues that "anyone leading mindfulness activities needs to have enough experience of the practices to be able to guide others in their own journey of introspection and support them when they encounter any obstacles."

However, Baer and Kuyken (2016) note that in reality, mindfulness meditation teacher training is in its infancy, and standards are less than ideal:

> Contemplative traditions have long recognized that intensive mindfulness practice can lead to challenging emotional or bodily experiences that require expert guidance. The developers of secular, evidence-based mindfulness programs also emphasize the

importance of competent mindfulness teaching. Unfortunately, interest in mindfulness classes has become so widespread that not enough qualified teachers are available. Some teachers have very little training and may be unprepared to help participants with either the normal and expected unpleasant experiences that arise or the more atypical unexpected side effects of mindfulness practice. They may do little screening and assessment to determine if people are suitable and ready for programmes at different levels of intensity. Teacher training programmes are themselves still developing, including with regard to how best to ensure the protection of those learning mindfulness. The field is only just beginning to develop good practice guidelines and listings of qualified teachers.

The authors also delineate different levels of mindfulness practice according to intensity, from low intensity (such as "bringing friendly awareness to the tastes and textures of food") to moderate intensity (techniques used in therapeutic mindfulness-based interventions) and high intensity practices (meditation retreats). While low to moderate intensity meditation practices are of less concern, particularly when taught in a one-on-one therapeutic relationship with a qualified medical professional, problems are more commonly reported in modern Western retreat settings. Baer and Kuyken write:

> The most intensive way to practice mindfulness is on meditation retreats, where participants typically meditate for many hours each day, often entirely in silence, for a week or more at a time. Contact with a teacher may occur only once every day or two. Most reports of adverse effects of mindfulness practice to date come from participants in intensive retreats. The best retreat centres are operated by meditation teachers with comprehensive knowledge of the retreat centre's orientation (e.g., Christian, Buddhist etc.), extensive experience in offering the teachings in those settings, and knowledge of the difficulties that may arise during intensive mindfulness practice. Teachers at these centres will frame the difficulties they encounter within their own orientation and experience and the best will undertake some degree of screening, have a safeguarding policy and ways of referring to treatment centres when appropriate.

Unfortunately not all meditation retreat centres are able to operate at such high standards, and extreme adverse events have been reported at, or following, some meditation retreats including rare cases of suicide (Vendel 2018). These extreme cases highlight another key factor that contributes to meditation adverse effects being overlooked: post-retreat follow-up. Many meditation adverse effects occur *after a retreat*, or "off-the-cushion," so may go unnoticed by teachers who are largely unavailable for practitioners to talk to post-retreat. Mark Epstein (2007: 14) notes that meditation teachers are in general not only untrained in psychotherapy and unprepared for the extreme distress that could arise in Western practitioners, but also uninterested in maintaining long-term personal relationships with students who might attend a workshop or retreat. Daniel Ingram also mentions this issue in *Mastering the Core Teachings of the Buddha*, noting that students are rarely able to engage in "comprehensive, deep conversations with harried and over-extended jet-set dharma teachers."

Scholars have argued that the quantity of media coverage about meditation in a variety of frames indicates a cultural acceptance of, and/or an active desire for information about, meditation (Lauricella 2014). As such, consumer demand for secular meditation is a trend that is likely to continue. Many people now seek meditation in highly variable settings both within and outside of clinical programs, and many individuals self-refer to meditation teachers and courses, often via the internet. Meditation teaching is currently an unregulated industry meaning that no prerequisite training standard for meditation teachers exists, and there are an unaccounted-for number of teachers who practise independently. As such, because meditation is fashionable at the moment, it may be taught by well-intentioned but inadequately trained teachers who have limited experience with meditation adverse effects. Hence, it is advisable that there is regulation around meditation teacher training, screening processes for potential or pre-existing psychopathology, ongoing support structures for potential meditation-related difficulties, and informed consent for meditation practitioners. As recognition and acceptance of the diversity of meditation experiences increases, it is hoped that meditation teachers and businesses will implement these standards and practices.

Individual differences and psychopathology

While transient adverse effects and difficulties integrating insights may occur as a normal part of meditation practice, it is also possible that some of the more extreme adverse effects that have recently been reported in the popular media are the result of an interaction between meditation practice and pre-existing or latent psychopathology. In Buddhist texts on meditation, there is recognition that not all meditation techniques will suit all individuals. For example, the *Visudhimagga* recommends forty different meditation subjects along with a variety of diverse physical surroundings that can be tailored to individual meditators:

> The lustful meditator, for example, should be assigned a cramped, windowless hut in an ugly location in the neighbourhood of unfriendly people; the hateful type, on the other hand, is to be given a comfortable and roomy cottage in a pleasant area near helpful people (Goleman 1988: 9).

Further, in some religious traditions it is understood that *meditation in general is not suited to every individual.* Some scholars have argued that traditionally physical and mental wellbeing, along with a stable personality, are prerequisites to meditation, and "troubled" people have been restricted from entering the practice (e.g. Awasthi 2103; Sedlmeier and Srinivas 2016). For example, regarding kundalini crisis, Sri Aurobindo (1872–1950) in *Letters on Yoga* writes that kundalini itself does not induce psychosis in previously healthy individuals. Rather kundalini crisis is the result of a constitutionally weak nervous system that is already predisposed to emotional problems and hence decompensates under the stress of a kundalini awakening. Psychotic decompensation due to kundalini awakening may therefore be less common in cultures and contexts where proper screening and preparation are prerequisites for yogic training (Greyson 1993).

Additionally, psychological therapy is not an explicit concern in Buddhism or Hinduism, and meditation in these traditions has not focused on an individual's personal history, emotions, or psychological issues. For example, despite the modern equation of suffering with psychopathology, depression in the clinical sense is not mentioned in Buddhist literature. The fifty-two mental factors of the *Abhidhamma* (third century BCE) list negative emotions such as greed, hatred, conceit, envy, doubt, worry, restlessness and avarice, but do not include sadness "except as a kind of unpleasant feeling that can tinge other mental states. Depression is not mentioned" (Epstein 2007: 144–45). Further, in the Tibetan Buddhist tradition, medical authorities recognise mental illnesses that correlate with Western diagnoses of depression, melancholia, panic, bipolar and psychosis, and for these they recommend pharmaceutical treatment, as it is understood that meditation can make these conditions worse (Epstein 2007: 149). While the Buddhist tradition holds that the ultimate cure for every kind of suffering is enlightenment, attainable through extensive meditation, Tibetan healing recommends against the use of meditation as a therapy for mental illness as it could lead to even greater anxiety (Benedict et al. 2009). Although this seems paradoxical, it points towards the diverse and complicated uses of meditation in various schools of Buddhism; meditation is understood to be able to both harm and heal.[37]

This is in direct contrast to how meditation is generally taught in contemporary secular Western settings. Today in the West, meditation is regularly used within the context of psychotherapy and meditators often come to the practice in search of psychological relief. However, more recent research is starting to reveal the complexities and problems associated with using meditation as a broad spectrum solution to treat psychopathology. For example, there is evidence to suggest that meditation may act as a stressor in psychologically vulnerable individuals. In *Psychotherapy without the Self*, Mark Epstein discusses unique meditation-related challenges that may arise for those with a diagnosis of borderline personality disorder, narcissistic personality disorder, schizoid personality, or depression. Other scholars have argued that meditation may be contraindicated in those who have obsessive-compulsive disorder (Didonna 2009), a history of trauma (Treleaven 2018), or who are emotionally fragile. For example, Germer (2005: 128)[38] argues that people who "decompensate when cognitive controls are loosened should generally not do formal sitting meditation" and that people with "fragile personalities" may benefit from learning meditation but duration of practice should be shortened. Didonna (2009) argues that individuals who suffer from pathological feelings of emptiness should also work with a therapist as meditation may lead to intense reactions such as dissociation, panic, or the need to escape. Additionally, the official standards of practice for mindfulness-based stress reduction (MBSR) state

---

[37] While an in-depth consideration of the treatment of mental illness in Buddhist traditions is beyond the scope of this book, a comprehensive discussion of meditation and mental illness can be found in Salguero's (2017) *Buddhism and Medicine: An Anthology of Premodern Sources*.

[38] Cited in Dobkin et al. (2012: 44).

that the treatment should exclude those who are suicidal or have a psychiatric disorder (Santorelli 2014).

As mentioned earlier, there has been a tendency in Western psychology to conflate meditation adverse effects with pre-existing or latent psychopathology. Indeed, one of the most difficult problems facing contemporary Western psychology may be how to dis-entangle "conventional suffering" (the suffering treated by psychotherapy and medicine) from the more existential distress that can occur as the result of meditation practice (for example, the experience of the *dukkha nanas* or the insight into emptiness) or specific meditation-related conditions (such as anxiety that is exacerbated by meditation). Attempts to resolve this issue may have to be informed by a more direct dialogue between religion and psychology. While consulting religious sources may prove controversial, and it is not recommended that classic meditation manuals are to be taken at face value, it is worth considering that a greater familiarity with the traditional literature may help to identify what adverse effects are normal and expected, how to deal with extreme or non-ordinary states of consciousness, how to distinguish meditation-related problems from psychopathology, and how to prevent unnecessary difficulties from occurring and escalating. This is an area that is ripe for future research.

CHAPTER SIX

"The answer to all your problems?" meditation and the media

> *You've got to accentuate the positive*
> *Eliminate the negative*
> *And latch on to the affirmative*
> *Don't mess with Mister In-Between*
> —"Ac-Cent-Tchu-Ate the Positive," Johnny Mercer 1944

All good news stories

The mainstream media represents a significant source of public knowledge about religion. In particular, scholars have argued that the media encourages the "deregulation" of religious ideas and symbols, allowing them to circulate throughout society in ways that are increasingly beyond the control of traditional religious institutions (Lynch et al. 2012: 1). One recent example of this type of deregulation is the popular media portrayal of meditation. Over the past half century, stories about Buddhist and Hindu-derived forms of meditation have saturated the Western mainstream media. While scholars of religion understand the word "meditation" to be an umbrella term that refers to a wide variety of contemplative practices that are situated within specific cultural contexts, meditation when referred to by the mainstream media is usually referring to Transcendental Meditation (TM) or mindfulness (which might include general mindfulness techniques, *vipassana* retreats or clinical mindfulness-based interventions). These are the specific types of meditation that have been studied the most by Western science and that have gained the most widespread mainstream popularity.

Mainstream media coverage of meditation gained traction in the late 1960s and 1970s when TM became popular with a number of celebrities including The Beatles. In 1975 *TIME* magazine ran a cover featuring an image of Maharishi Mahesh Yogi, the founder of TM, along with the headline: "Meditation: The Answer to All Your Problems?" More recently, "mindfulness" has become a popular media buzzword that has generated a huge amount of interest and enthusiasm and has permeated the discourse of popular culture (Sun 2014). In 2014 *TIME* magazine ran another meditation-related cover, this one titled "The Mindful Revolution" along with an accompanying story detailing the extent to which mindfulness meditation has spread into the largest sectors of modern Western society. In the same year the *Huffington Post*, a popular American news site which has its own Mindfulness news section, declared 2014 the "Year of Mindful Living." Since the late 1970s in particular, there has been a significant proliferation of meditation-related news articles, indicating an increased interest in meditation practice (Lauricella 2014).

Alongside the popular news coverage of meditation there has been a growing concern, particularly among the scientific community, that the media portrayal of meditation is incomplete and at times inaccurate. In particular, there appears to be a disconnect between scientific research on meditation and media reporting, and many news stories fail to accurately present research, exaggerate the benefits of meditation, and ignore potential adverse effects.

An analysis of media news stories about meditation reveals a clear positivity bias. For example, a recent study by Sharon Lauricella (2014) analysed 764 mainstream print media articles about meditation that were published between 1979 and 2014. Lauricella used frame theory analysis to understand how meditation is presented in print media. The study found that almost half of the news stories analysed spoke of meditation's positive effects on physical ailments (such as asthma, headaches, chronic pain, inflammation, and cardiovascular disease), and 88% spoke of the emotional benefits of meditation (including improvements in work relationships and family life, greater empathy and sensitivity, an increased sense of calm, and stress relief). From the sample of articles, only six reported on negative aspects of meditation.

What are the factors that have led to such an overwhelmingly positive portrayal of meditation in the media? Specifically, a portrayal that ignores some of the possible limitations of meditation, including potential difficulties and adverse effects?

Meditation tropes

An analysis of the popular media coverage of meditation reveals several reoccurring motifs or "tropes." One particularly common trope is the conceptualisation of meditation as a form of spiritual or mental hygiene. Lauricella (2014: 1748) posits that popular news articles about meditation "reflect the health and wellness challenges present in contemporary culture, together with a desire for personal relief from such issues." Following this, she suggests that her data support the conceptualisation of meditation as a form of "spiritual hygiene"; that is, a spiritual practice that, like physical hygiene, can relieve the practitioner of negative effects "much like brushing one's teeth reduces the likelihood of cavities, washing the body prevents infections and unpleasant odours, and grooming the body assists in one's overall sense of wellness and confidence" (Lauricella 2014: 1758). However, unlike physical hygiene practices, spiritual hygiene also serves an additional and greater salvific function as a method for returning a practitioner to "wholeness." A more secular adaptation of this trope is "mental hygiene" or "brain hygiene." For example, an article on the popular website *Psychology Today* notes: "Meditation is quite simply mental hygiene: clear out the junk, tune your talents, and get in touch with yourself. Think about it, you shower every day and clean your body, but have you ever showered your mind?" (Seppälä 2013). Examples of meditation presented as a form of mental hygiene or brain hygiene can be found throughout the popular news media (e.g. Kelsey-Sugg and Zajac 2018; Pflugshaupt 2018).

Meditation is also portrayed by the media as a pathway to happiness, and recent popular news headlines include "How Meditation Increases Happiness" (Cho 2016), "The Science Behind Why Meditation Makes You So Much Happier" (Schwartz 2018), and "Grow Your

Own Happiness: How Meditation Physically Changes the Brain" (Knapton 2015). This trend has likely been informed by the "happiness turn" of the past two decades, whereby the scientific study of happiness has become a popular research topic and has been widely reported on in the mass media (Ahmed 2007). The science of meditation and happiness is now cited frequently in contemporary discussions of both happiness and meditation, particularly in popular presentations of secular Buddhist-derived forms of meditation such as mindfulness (Edelglass 2017). Scholar Robert Sharf (2015: 472) argues that in the West, Buddhism itself is now commonly seen as a "science of happiness" and "Buddhist practice is reduced to meditation, and meditation, in turn, is reduced to mindfulness, which is touted as a therapeutic practice that leads to an emotionally fulfilling and rewarding life."

Well-known spiritual leaders and meditation teachers are also promoted by the popular media as symbols of happiness. For example, TM founder Maharishi Mahesh Yogi was dubbed "the giggling guru" by the media, and news stories often featured images of Mahesh laughing (Shunsky 2018). More recently, French-born Buddhist monk Matthieu Ricard has been referred to by journalists as "the happiest person in the world" (Barnes 2007). Ricard has been given this title because brain scans have reportedly demonstrated excessive activity in his brain's left prefrontal cortex, indicating an abnormally large capacity for experiencing happiness and a reduced tendency towards negativity. However, Ricard himself says that while he is a generally happy person, the title "happiest person in the world" is a media-driven headline that he finds "absurd" (Paterniti 2016). Regardless of the truth behind such claims, these types of exaggerated headlines bestow scientific authority onto the idea that meditation increases happiness, and "increased happiness" has become one of the key ways in which meditation is marketed.

Finally, perhaps the most common image associated with meditation in the popular media is that of the "tranquil meditator." Scott Mitchell (2014) coined this term to describe a reoccurring character in American media representations of Buddhism. The tranquil meditator is usually presented as Western, often female, seated in some version of the lotus position, and meditating by herself in solitude. Variations of this image have been used on two *TIME* magazine covers (2003 and 2014) and appear regularly in the stock image photos that accompany stories about meditation on popular news sites such as the *Huffington Post* (e.g. Campbell 2017; Dissanayaka 2018) and *Forbes* (Kaplan 2017).

Mitchell argues that this character points towards a "vague and ill-defined Asian spirituality or mysticism that is directly tied to a calm, centering, and relaxed state of mind" (Mitchell 2014: 84). Hence, the tranquil meditator trope reinforces the popular mainstream view of meditation as a seated practice that is associated with happiness and relaxation, and engaged in for secular pragmatic purposes such as improved health and wellness.

Scientist-journalist communication

While it is true that numerous scientific studies have shown a correlation between some specific meditation practices and increased levels of happiness, relaxation, and wellbeing, the view of meditation that is portrayed by the Western media is radically simplified and incomplete. Specifically, it is an overwhelmingly positive view, which at its most extreme, promotes meditation as a type of panacea or cure-all (e.g. Drougge 2016: 170–71). In particular, popular news stories about meditation tend to exaggerate the positive outcomes from scientific studies and obscure the challenges that occur in meditation research. As mentioned earlier, there are many methodological issues in meditation research, including small sample sizes, inadequate control groups, demographic homogeneity among participants, inattention to gender as a variable, difficulties in operationally defining "meditation", and limitations regarding technology such as magnetic resonance imaging (MRI) and magnetoencephalography (e.g. Van Dam et al. 2018). While such problems are not limited to meditation research, and are in fact common to psychological science and neuroscience in general, the media's disregard of these issues has led to two very different discourses regarding meditation: scientific consensus and the popular press coverage regarding that consensus.

Scholars have argued that the disparity between what meditation research actually demonstrates and what is presented in the media is partly due to communication issues between scientists and journalists. Eklöf (2016) notes that over the past thirty years, science (in the form of scientific organisations and their members) has developed a closer relationship with the mass media, and is more responsive to the priorities and needs of media organisations. Additionally, with the more recent growth of online media, there has been an increasing personalisation of scientific communication, whereby scientists can bypass traditional media channels and convey information directly to the public via their own personal websites, blogs, and social media networks. In these more direct personal media channels, content is controlled by the scientist-communicator, who can avoid the regular barriers associated with specialist communication with the mass media. As a result, the tone of this type of communication is often more conversational, and there may be an emphasis on pragmatic applications and personal experiences, rather than sophisticated discussions of published research findings (Eklöf 2016).

In the case of mindfulness research, it has been noted that many scientists in this area have a "double identity" both as scientists and practitioners of the meditation techniques that they study (Parsons 2009; Wilson 2014). Further, these scientists may differ in their professional and popular communications regarding mindfulness. For example, the research literature suggests there is a lot of uncertainty concerning the benefits of mindfulness meditation, and studies often emphasise the existence of knowledge gaps, poor methodological design, and the preliminary nature of many research findings. Further, where positive psychological and physiological effects of mindfulness are reported, the neural mechanisms underlying these effects are still regarded as being largely unknown and poorly understood, and researchers admit that the neuroscientific study of meditation is "still in its infancy" (Eklöf 2016: 327). Hence, academic papers on mindfulness commonly point out methodological flaws and limitations, and call for more methodologically rigorous studies. However, this level of uncertainty is not present to the same degree in more personalised, popular scientific accounts of mindfulness meditation, which generally give the impression that mindfulness is unquestionably effective. Eklöf (2016: 327) notes that popular scientific accounts often emphasise the "revolutionary" and "cutting-edge" nature of meditation research, and suggest that with neuroscientific studies of meditation, we are "witnessing something like a paradigmatic revolution in science and medicine." Rather than pointing out limitations, popular accounts of mindfulness use science as a symbol of validity; self-help books, blog posts, and websites commonly note that mindfulness meditation is "science based" and has been tested in the "rigorous" setting of the neuroscience laboratory (Eklöf 2016: 327).

Further, a common theme that runs throughout the popular scientific mindfulness literature is that meditation practice is an integral part of the lives of those conducting or communicating the research. Eklöf (2016: 329) cites the example of Richard Davidson's book *The Emotional Life of Your Brain*, in which the author recounts his own personal story of "coming out of the closet" as a meditator, and his "personal and scientific transformation" as a result of meditation practice. The field of meditation, by definition, places a unique status on experiential knowledge, and such personal endorsements from highly accomplished and esteemed scientists are often taken at face value. Hence, they provide a level of perceived legitimacy to the effectiveness of meditation while deflecting attention away from the shortcomings of actual scientific research.

In the recent article "Mind the Hype," Van Dam et al. (2018: 51) call for more truth in advertising from meditation researchers, particularly regarding the limitations of mindfulness studies. However, even when scientists do caution about the limitations of scientific studies and the preliminary nature of research findings, journalists seeking a sensational headline may still cherry pick research that supports their specific agenda, or greatly oversimplify scientific studies. One study that has received a large amount of media attention is the paper by Sara Lazar et al. (2005), "Meditation Experience Is Associated with Increased Cortical Thickness." While the findings from this paper were preliminary, scholars have argued that it was over-hyped by the media (Heuman 2014). For example, an article in the *Daily Mail* (titled "Proof that Meditation CAN Grow Your Brain: In Just Eight Weeks It Can Improve Learning and Memory") cites Lazar's work (but does not mention the specific study) as evidence that meditation can "strengthen" the brain and "make the brain bigger" (Adams 2014). Examples such as these demonstrate how oversimplified reporting of meditation research findings can result in captivating news headlines, but also lead to exaggerated (and at times nonsensical) claims that are not supported by the underlying science.

Further, sensational news stories about meditation tend to get circulated virally via social media channels and repetition is often conflated with validity. As neuroscientist Catherine Kerr (1964–2016) has written:

> The Huffington Post is the worst offender. The message they deliver becomes a ubiquitous, circulating meme that people put up on their Facebook pages and that becomes "true" through repetition alone. The Huffington Post features mindfulness a lot and tends to

represent only the positive findings (and in the most positive light imaginable) rather than offering a balanced reading of the science (Heuman 2014).

In terms of real-world effects, scholars have argued that the exaggeration of meditation's benefits may lead to an "undue societal urgency" to take up meditation practices (Van Dam et al. 2018: 50). Specifically, overly simplified media-reporting may mislead people into thinking that meditation is a broad-based panacea, when, in fact, specific interventions may only be helpful for particular people in certain circumstances. As a result, meditation could be viewed as more effective than it really is, or utilised for conditions that it was never designed to treat. Hence, people who self-diagnose based on media reports, and seek meditation to treat unrelated problems, may be at best wasting their time and money, and at worst, putting themselves at risk of adverse effects (Van Dam et al. 2018). Most worryingly, when the media portrays meditation as a universal cure-all, it can lead people to abandon effective and appropriate medical treatments and replace them with untested meditation practices. Kerr says:

> I've heard reports of people who have abandoned chemotherapy to do mindfulness. I don't know if that has really happened. Certainly there are people who go off their antidepressants or lithium and think that mindfulness is going to manage their serious depression or bipolar disorder. That's a concern we have with the current hype around mindfulness. People might see it as being more active than it really is. It doesn't resolve those situations (Heuman 2014).

Sensationalistic reporting on meditation may lead to the creation of larger problems for meditation-based interventions and the general image of meditation. Specifically, there is the risk that misinformation and excessive hype could eventually lead to a backlash and widespread public mistrust of meditation. Indeed, the few popular news headlines regarding possible adverse effects of meditation have been equally as sensationalist as the positive ones. Recent examples from major news sites include "What Mindfulness Gurus Won't Tell You: Meditation Has a Dark Side" (Farias and Wikholm 2016), "Is Mindfulness Making Us Ill?" (Foster 2016), and "Dangers of Meditation" (Ivtzan 2016). While sensationalist stories that promote meditation as a cure-all may result in adverse effects for some specific groups, headlines that promote fearmongering at the expense of informed debate could equally lead to adverse effects, in that many people who might actually benefit from meditation could miss out. Hence, balanced media reporting on meditation reduces harm for all involved.

Celebrity gurus and celebrity meditators

The familiarisation and positive reception of meditation in the West has been heavily facilitated by celebrity influence. From the late nineteenth century to the present, meditation has had a strong association with celebrity, in the form of both celebrity gurus and celebrity meditators. The Theosophical Society, one of the earliest Western promoters of Eastern meditation, was founded in New York in 1875 by Helena Petrovna Blavatsky (1831–1891) and Colonel Henry Steel Olcott (1832–1907), who were both celebrities of the era (Cusack 2011). Western meditation narratives have also tended to focus on charismatic spiritual gurus and meditation teachers such as Maharishi Mahesh Yogi (1918–2008), Bhagwan Shree Rajneesh (also known as Osho; 1931–1990), Daisetz T. Suzuki (1870–1966), Chogyam Trungpa (1939–1987), and His Holiness Tenzin Gyatso, the Fourteenth Dalai Lama. These individuals have been portrayed by the media as exceptional characters, endowed with extraordinary qualities, and have become celebrities themselves (Borup 2016).

TM in particular has had a large celebrity following which began with The Beatles (Goldberg 2010), and has continued more recently with Hollywood filmmaker David Lynch (who has established a charitable foundation dedicated to fund the teaching of TM) and other high-profile celebrity supporters including Katy Perry (Gander 2018), Hugh Jackman (Rosenthal 2016), Naomi Watts (Pringle 2015), Moby, Russell Brand and Jerry Seinfeld (Aleksander 2011). In 2003, actress Goldie Hawn founded The Hawn Foundation, which teaches mindfulness practices to children; she has also published three popular books on mindfulness (Wilson 2014: 58–59). Meditation is also reportedly popular amongst athletes (Dulaney 2018) and high-profile CEOs, including Rupert Murdoch, who in 2013 tweeted that he was "trying to learn transcendental meditation" (Colgan 2013). Scientists themselves—usually white, male, middle-class American neuroscientists, such as Richard Davidson and Rick Hanson—have also become popular celebrity figures.

The majority of these celebrities promote meditation as a secular practice, removed from any particular religion. Popular celebrity accounts of meditation are also focused on success stories—how meditation has contributed to increased health, happiness and success—and not stories of how meditation has been challenging or has failed people.

The reason this is of interest is because celebrities are important sources of influence, and hence affect the way that meditation is represented and understood in contemporary Western society. Historically, news coverage of celebrities was mainly confined to tabloids, magazines, and special sections of newspapers. However today, with the recent democratisation of the media and the rise of the twenty-four-hour news cycle, celebrity news is a widespread phenomenon and can be found across the entire media landscape. Scholars have argued that celebrity news has become pervasive to the extent that it constitutes a "new normal," and stories about celebrities are often presented in the popular media as if they were as significant as traditional news stories (Dubied and Hanitzsch 2014). Because of their fame, celebrities are able to spotlight issues; that is, they generate large amounts of attention and publicity due to their high visibility, public interest, and the perceived newsworthiness of their message. In addition to being able to gain the public's attention, studies have shown that messages delivered by well-known celebrities also achieve a high degree of recall for some consumers and hence may lead to an increased intention to purchase a celebrity-endorsed product or service (Ohanian 1991).

Additionally, when celebrities speak about issues they often have a level of credibility and influence that rivals or exceeds traditional sources including scientists, politicians and medical professionals (Harvey 2017). Celebrities may be such successful influencers because consumers see in them attributes they admire and want to emulate. For many people, celebrities possess attractive qualities and high status, and represent important social or cultural meanings. Marketing researchers posit that a celebrity's attractive qualities are symbolically transferred to the product they endorse, making it appear more desirable; a process that marketers refer to as "meaning transfer" (Hoffman and Tan 2015). People will then consume the product in the hopes of acquiring those same positive traits. Some researchers have also described a "halo effect" whereby the predominant positive trait of a celebrity biases how all their other traits and behaviours are perceived (Hoffman and Tan 2015). This combination of high visibility and high influence explains how celebrities successfully persuade audiences and directly influence public opinion and behaviour, including health-related behaviours (Stevens and Rusby 2014). Hence, celebrities can be powerful agents in the dissemination of information, and celebrity endorsement is a highly effective vehicle for the positive promotion and mainstreaming of meditation techniques. While celebrity endorsement of meditation is no doubt well-meaning, the combined factors of high visibility and influence, perceived credibility, and ubiquitously positive content all contribute to an overly positive view of meditation in the popular media.

Meditation for sale

Scholars have argued that the influence of organised religion is declining in many Western nations (e.g. Altemeyer 2004). Simultaneously, there has been a growing commercialisation of religion in the form of "spirituality," resulting in the emergence of what has been called a "spiritual marketplace" (Carrette and King 2005) and an enthusiasm on the part of the public to learn how to alleviate personal and health problems with techniques that are "spiritual but not religious" (Lauricella 2014: 1760). As such, a variety of commodified forms of "secular" meditation-related businesses and services have emerged to service this multi-million dollar market (Gelles 2016). As discussed earlier, there is much debate regarding whether meditation can ever be truly secular (e.g. Gunther Brown 2016), however for the purposes of this book, secular meditation refers to meditation techniques that are marketed as non-religious; that is, "stripped both of religious beliefs and cultural specifics" (Drougge 2016: 169). Secular meditation-related businesses and services tend to promote meditation, via the popular media and their own personal websites and social media, as a type of panacea that is harmless, suitable for anyone, and helpful for a variety of personal issues.

Outside of the purely clinical domain, mainstream commodified meditation is generally presented as a technique for either self-care or self-improvement. In medicine, the term "self-care" originated in reference to the self-management of illness; namely, its treatment and prevention. However, more recently the term has become a popular buzzword used to refer to a variety of democratised strategies for attending to the self, with the goal of maintaining or optimising health. The discourse around self-care has emerged as part of a broader Western cultural interest in wellness, indicated by a collective shift away from total reliance on the medical establishment in matters of health, and toward the idea that the individual can take responsibility for their own wellbeing. This interest in wellness and self-care is reflected in the current contemporary Western fascination with natural products, and the rising popularity of complementary and alternative medicine (e.g. Gunther Brown 2013). Within this context, meditation is often presented as a self-care practice, similar to engaging in regular exercise.

In the spiritual marketplace, secular meditation is also promoted as a tool for self-improvement. Self-improvement is a dominant narrative in modern Western culture, and the idea of bettering oneself, often in relation to one's resilience and productivity, is central to contemporary Western neoliberal values. The link between meditation and self-improvement can be traced back to early interactions between Buddhism and the West. For example, Richard Payne (2016: 126) posits that since its earliest introduction into Western society, Buddhism has been integrated as a form of self-improvement. He writes:

> The culture of self-improvement has appropriated Buddhism as a part of a century and a half long fascination with the exotic in general, and the "Mystic East" and its "ancient wisdom" in particular. And, Euro-American proponents of Buddhism have themselves made use of the self-improvement culture as a ready-made vehicle for promoting Buddhism. Some might justify this by claiming that since the origins in the sangha that formed around Śākyamuni, Buddhism has been a self-improvement program, or perhaps even the original self-improvement program.

While no longer explicitly linked to Buddhism, secular commodified forms of meditation are now frequently presented as tools or resources upon which people can draw in order to improve themselves and their lives. A variety of coaches, counsellors, and personal trainers all sell secular meditation-based products and services, and popular self-improvement tropes position meditation as a form of "mind hacking" or "mental fitness" (Tlalka 2018). Secular meditation is particularly prevalent in the "life hacking" or "quantified self" movements, where individuals track various aspects of their lives in order to improve or "hack" them (Wexler 2017). For example, at the time of writing, a search for the term "meditation" on the blog of popular performance-improvement entrepreneur and "biohacker" Dave Asprey returned 443 results.[39] According to a *New York Times* magazine article titled "You, Only Better," Asprey travelled to Tibet to study meditation as part of his own campaign of self-improvement (Wortham 2015).

The association between meditation and "mental fitness" is also a common theme in the commodified meditation space, with analogies often being drawn between mental fitness and physical fitness. For example, an article on meditation website Headspace notes:

> like physical fitness, mind fitness can be strengthened through attention and concentration practices (i.e. meditation) that literally change the brain structurally and functionally—a process called neuroplasticity. Just like you build up muscle strength to prevent injury or weakness, mind fitness builds resiliency that leads to faster recovery from psychological stress … Think of it like hitting the gym (Aguirre 2015).

In this context meditation is practised in the pursuit of mental strength and resilience; it is a tool for dealing with the demands of stress, and a technique for developing attention, concentration and self-discipline, which can then enhance productivity.

There are two obvious issues related to the commodification of meditation that are directly relevant to the question of why meditation has been presented so positively in the mainstream media. The first is that of power and influence; successful meditation teachers and meditation businesses with large marketing budgets are able to direct the popular media discourse surrounding meditation via their marketing and public relations efforts, which then shape the thoughts and perceptions of the general public. The second issue is that of profit; simply put, it is commercially advantageous for meditation teachers and businesses to present meditation in an overly positive way in order to gain business. A basic consequence of "meditation for sale" is that meditation-related businesses exist primarily to make revenue. While these businesses may profess their desire to alleviate suffering, help others or change the world, the potential for profit is generally the primary motive for any entrepreneurial activity. As one of the few recent news articles

---

[39] *Bulletproof Blog*, https://blog.bulletproof.com/. Accessed December 2018.

on meditation's adverse effects notes: "Meditation and mindfulness are big business, and distressed meditators aren't a good sales pitch" (Lauder 2018). The article goes on to cite scholar Willoughby Britton, who suggests that commercial interests might be a contributing factor in the underreporting of meditation's adverse effects: "One of the teachers told me that it's not good advertising to talk about these side-effects, so it has been under-reported," Willoughby said (Lauder 2018).

However, it is also possible that meditation businesses communicate an overly positive image of meditation simply due to a lack of deep knowledge and experience regarding meditation practices. A large part of the appeal of popular mainstream forms of meditation is that they are usually presented as being secular, or unassociated with any formal religion. This distancing from religion is understandable, given that connecting meditation to religious origins could severely limit the generalisation and acceptance of the practices in healthcare, education and other secular areas. However, it also means that vital information is lost. Specifically, in the Eastern contemplative traditions the goal of meditation is enlightenment, and the religious lineages from which popular meditation practices derive all warn about possible problems associated with meditation. In particular, meditation's adverse effects are well-known and acknowledged within certain Buddhist and Hindu yogic lineages. Meditation manuals, spiritual autobiographies and literature on stages of the path note that meditation adverse effects may arise simply as a normal stage on the path of progress towards enlightenment, or if the practice is not undertaken with adequate preparation, in the right conditions, and with proper guidance from a qualified teacher (Lutkajtis 2018).

However, in the mainstream meditation marketplace it is often the businesses that are the most successful at marketing that succeed, not necessarily the ones that are the most well-informed. As Jeff Wilson (2016: 119) notes:

> Quality control becomes ever harder to enforce as profits accrue to those who can best gain customers through savvy marketing and product design—these do not necessarily mean that the products are of low quality, but customers flock to products that have the slickest ads or apps with the nicest interface, which are not guaranteed to be those with the most reliable instructors or deepest understanding of meditation.

In commercial environments the highly experienced and ordained meditation teacher is frequently being replaced by instructors who come from a variety of spiritual, personal development and other backgrounds. Anyone can call themselves a meditation teacher, and business acumen may be more relevant than years of personal meditation experience or deep knowledge regarding the complexities of practice. An online search for meditation teacher training courses reveals a variety of courses ranging from four days to six weeks or more in duration. In these settings knowledge regarding meditation's adverse effects may be unknown and remain uncommunicated.

How should meditation be portrayed?

What would a more accurate media portrayal of meditation actually look like? Moreover, can anything ever be "accurately" portrayed by the media? The study of media technology over the past fifty years has highlighted the role of the media in shaping the way information is received, processed, and assimilated by an audience. Scholars of media and religion have noted that the communications technologies we use are not simply neutral channels that can be used to objectively transmit a message of our choice. Rather, the media actively shapes religious ideas and behaviours in particular ways, and has, to some degree, the power to determine which ideas will succeed and which will go unnoticed. Hence, the media not only reports on culture; to an extent it also shapes culture (Veidlinger 2018: 4). Additionally, new forms of media (particularly digital media) result in new ways of thinking about, relating to, and practising religion and religious-derived techniques such as meditation (Mahan 2014: 36). Whether new media technologies cause these changes in thinking and behaviour or simply allow them to emerge is largely indeterminable. What is clear, however, is that mainstream understandings of meditation have been significantly shaped by its portrayal in the popular media.

While media-audience relationships are complex and symbiotic, the issues that have been raised in this chapter are not reflective of best practice or balanced media reporting. The use of oversimplification, exaggeration, and "churnalism" (public relations disguised as news), while seemingly inherent to how the mass media operates today, often results in biased and parochial worldviews (Ward 2013: 2). This problem is not unique to media reporting on religion or meditation per se. Nor does it necessarily apply only to positive portrayals of meditation; reports on meditation's adverse effects are also sometimes sensationalised.

A more accurate portrayal of meditation might, as a start, consist of less reliance on problematic and outdated tropes, more accurate reporting by journalists, a more critical approach to the epistemological claims made by "celebrity" meditators, and a more balanced consideration of the wide diversity of meditation practices, practitioners, and experiences. Such a portrayal of meditation is likely to reveal a highly complex and culturally specific practice that is not easily packaged for commercial consumption.

It is also important to note there are benefits to the current digital media landscape, including an enhanced opportunity for back-and-forth dialogue, and a much greater questioning of authority. For example, Veidlinger (2018: 8) argues that "the two-way information flow enabled by the Internet can foster greater criticism and lead to challenges from below to those on top who had in the past monopolised access to the mass media." Indeed, there is evidence to suggest that in our current digital society, fewer people now submit completely to the authority of a religion or spiritual practice. Instead, they regard themselves as holding the authority to decide what they accept and reject from a tradition and how they choose to practise (Mahan 2014: 36). This focus on dialogue and the questioning of traditional authority structures can be seen in online meditation communities such as the Dharma Overground, Awake Network and the Hamilton project, all of which have a transparent "open access" approach to meditation information (Gleig 2019: 129–135).

CHAPTER SEVEN

Facing the shadow

> *I welcome it (the shadow) as an historic and necessary rectification of almost incalculable importance. For it forces us to accept a philosophical relativism such as Einstein embodies for mathematical physics, and which is fundamentally a truth of the Far East whose ultimate effects we cannot at present foresee.*
>
> —C.G. Jung.[40]

The denial of the dark side

One of the issues that intrigued me most regarding my meditation adverse effects research was the resistance I encountered from some members of the secular meditation community. In particular, a very small number of meditation teachers expressed obvious discomfort (and sometimes outright denial) regarding the idea that there could be anything "dark" about meditation. This discomfort and denial usually manifested in the form of victim blaming. If there was a meditation-related problem, then it was generally attributed to the individual meditator; they were "doing it wrong," practising too much, were

---

[40] C.G. Jung, *The Collected Works. Volume I–XX*. Edited by Sir Herbert Read. 2014: 7348.

depressed, had a personality disorder, the list goes on. It seemed that for some people, meditation occupied an unchallengeable position. It was unquestionably good. Hence, a question that I was faced with early on in my research was: *what does it mean when something is held to be "all good"?*

In *Practice and All Is Coming*, a study of sexual and physical abuse in the global Ashtanga yoga community, Matthew Remski (2019: 54) describes how spiritual practices that are idealised and promoted as "all good" may be hiding a shadow side. He notes:

> The benefits of Jois's Ashtanga yoga are lauded in countless books, blogs, podcasts, and videos. The method has been said to cure all manner of diseases, from the physical to the spiritual. Such idealization is a red flag. If anyone speaks of their teacher, method, or community in all-good terms, it's an invitation to look a little deeper.

To put it bluntly, when a spiritual practice is framed in "all good" terms, it is likely that someone is trying to sell you something. Remski (2019: 54) describes how the desire to influence and coerce can underlie "all good" narratives:

> They [all-good narratives] can also be features of any system that seeks to grow its influence. If a community presents its method or leadership in unqualified positive terms, they're not just expressing devotion. They are inviting you to get closer, to join up, to buy something. If you are already in the group, they might be trying to get you to stay.

In some spiritual contexts, all good narratives may be indicative of a "self-sealing" group or system. The term "self-sealed" comes from Janja Lalich's work on cultic dynamics and refers to a group that is closed off from outside influences and where members of the group are locked into a "bounded reality"—a system where everything is narrativised and interpreted to suit the needs of the group and the group's leader (e.g. Lalich and McLaren 2017). Any information that challenges or disconfirms the validity of the system, or that might cause internal dissent, is not allowed. My own research did not explicitly address the role of cultic dynamics in meditation groups and organisations, but this is an area that certainly warrants further attention.

Spiritual bypassing

As an audience, individuals in the modern West are particularly receptive to "all good" ideas and messages. A willingness to idealise meditation may result from longing and sentimentality—the desire for a perfect solution to all of our problems. Indeed, many scholars have attempted to explain the West's attraction to Eastern spiritual practices as being due to disenchantment with the limits of Western medicine, a fascination with romanticised New Age orientalism, and a desire to find a substitute for the meaning and solace that was once found (but now seems to be increasingly lost in this secular age) in traditional religion. The denial of a dark side to meditation may also stem from our culture's current fixation on the positive; from a New Age milieu that promotes manifestation and prosperity consciousness, to "positive psychology" and the "happiness turn" of the past two decades (e.g. Ahmed 2007), there has been an explosion of interest in concepts such as "wellbeing," "self-care" and "positive neuroplasticity." It seems that as human beings, we are hardwired for hope; we want to believe that we can positively shape our individual and collective futures. However, at its most extreme, this fixation on the positive can express itself as an unrealistic denial and rejection of anything perceived as being too "negative" or challenging to face.

In spiritual-psychological contexts, an overemphasis on the positive and a devaluation or repression of the negative has been described as "spiritual bypassing." This term was first introduced in 1984 by John Welwood (1943–2019), a psychologist, psychotherapist and prominent figure in transpersonal psychology. Welwood coined the term in order to describe a common pattern he was noticing among Western spiritual seekers who were using spiritual philosophies and practices to avoid dealing with unresolved psychological issues. In *Toward a Psychology of Awakening*, Welwood (2000: 12) notes "I call this tendency to avoid or prematurely transcend basic human needs, feelings, and developmental tasks *spiritual bypassing*."

Spiritual bypassing is generally used to describe a personal process, however it can also be used to explain behaviours that occur on a collective level. In *Spiritual Bypassing*, Robert Augustus Masters (2010: 1–2) argues that as a culture we have a low tolerance for facing and working through existential and psychological pain. Instead, we prefer pain-numbing "solutions" which can manifest as spiritual bypassing:

> Because this preference [to avoid pain] has so deeply and thoroughly infiltrated our culture that it has become all but normalized, spiritual bypassing fits almost seamlessly into our collective habit of turning away from what is painful, as a kind of higher analgesic with seemingly minimal side effects. It is a spiritualized strategy not only for avoiding pain but also for legitimizing such avoidance, in ways ranging from the blatantly obvious to the extremely subtle.

An example of collective spiritual bypassing is the widespread denial or avoidance of the dark side of meditation. One way this manifests is as a preoccupation with the attainment of pleasant meditative states (such as calm abiding or relaxation) and the avoidance or repression of difficult or challenging meditative experiences. In spiritual bypassing, "negative" emotions (such as fear, anger, sadness or disgust) are not acknowledged because they do not align with the ideal spiritual persona that an individual is trying to cultivate. When this splitting of "positive" and "negative" cognitions and emotions occurs, the individual loses the opportunity to use challenging thoughts and feelings in order to work on unresolved psychological issues (Welwood 2011). Similarly, in modern meditation contexts, negative content (such as difficult thoughts, emotions, or physical sensations) and challenging experiences are often minimised, treated superficially or invalidated. For example, a common instruction given to meditators is to simply "just sit" and "observe" any challenging sensations that arise, and to continue to practise through any difficulties. Such instructions are designed to help the meditation practitioner overcome experiential avoidance, however this is not always an appropriate instruction for everyone, all of the time. Specifically, Treleaven (2018) argues that for individuals with a history of trauma, paying attention to unpleasant trauma-related sensations (such as stomach clenching or flashbacks) might exacerbate and entrench these symptoms. In such situations, simply observing in silence may be a harmful response, and the meditator might be better served by ceasing practice and seeking an alternative therapy.

Adverse effects can also occur when meditation is used to replace psychotherapy. Psychotherapy, in the sense that it is understood in the

West, is not significantly addressed in most traditional religious or spiritual paths. While some streams of contemporary spirituality do recognise that there are particular problems that spirituality may not be able to adequately address, such as severe biologically based mental illnesses, Western psychotherapy is a relatively recent cultural development that was not included in Eastern contemplative traditions. For example, in *A Path With Heart*, Jack Kornfield has acknowledged that at least half of the Western students who undertake three-month *vipassana* retreats at the Insight Meditation Society are unable to continue with practice because they encounter so many emotional and psychological issues that cannot be resolved simply by meditating. However, with spiritual bypassing there is a tendency to devalue the personal and interpersonal relative to the spiritual. This is evident when psychotherapy is deemed inferior to "spiritual work" since it concerns and supports the "ego" self—the very thing that meditative practice is trying to eradicate. Thus, spiritual bypassing frequently presents as the belief that if an individual practises meditation diligently enough, they can "transcend" their egoic self and all its related mundane psychological problems. Masters (2010: 29) describes how spiritual bypassing involves privileging transcendence and "making a spiritual virtue out of rising above whatever is deemed 'lower' or 'darker.'" He writes:

> Descending into our darker elements may be construed as a "downer" or a slippage, a failure, a dropping into the "lower." We tend to either pathologize down-ness (especially when it shows up as negativity, fear, depression, shame, or contraction) or keep it at a considerable distance, as if it is just some sort of noxious or unwholesome substance … Viewing being down (as when we are depressed or in turmoil) as something negative, something far from spiritual, turns being up (as when we are on a roll or are immersed in being positive) into an exaggeratedly important quality, to be held aloft even when circumstances clearly call for something very different … (Masters 2010: 30).

Indeed, the "something very different" that is required may involve ceasing contemplative practice altogether and engaging in psychotherapy. Alternately, it may entail a change in meditation practice type, frequency or duration. Regardless, when negative content is minimised, treated cursorily, or simply avoided it can exacerbate meditation adverse effects.

Spiritual bypassing may also present as a lack of critical thinking in otherwise rational individuals. For example, a popular definition of mindfulness meditation is "paying attention in a particular way: on purpose, in the present moment, and non-judgmentally" (Kabat-Zinn 1994: 4). However, a fixation on the positive, combined with excessive cultivation of non-judgment, can lead to a loss of rationality—what Masters (2010: 145) has referred to as "spiritual gullibility" or cultism. When it comes to meditation practice, a level of healthy judgment and discernment is both necessary and useful. For example, critical judgment is required in order to determine whether a particular meditation practice feels right or is getting the desired results. Circumstances may call for a practice to be adapted or to be stopped altogether. Highly intelligent and otherwise rational individuals might persist with practices that harm them, such as continuing to attempt to sit in full lotus despite having a knee injury. Others continue with practices that don't seem to be providing any benefit but they choose to persist due to blind faith in the teacher or the prescribed path. Discernment is also required in order to differentiate between metaphysical and worldly layers of truth and reality. For example, spiritual bypassing may involve "magical thinking." In the case of meditation this may manifest as the belief that with enough intentionality and focus we can bypass the laws of reality. I recall once asking a highly regarded meditation teacher why meditation was not curing my chronic pain. He replied: "*Meditation is not magic.*" At the time, I was so steeped in the popular messaging around the alleged all-powerful healing properties of this particular style of meditation that this answer genuinely surprised and disappointed me.

At its worst, spiritual bypassing involves the use of spiritual beliefs and philosophies to justify, and hence bypass, issues of abuse and injustice in spiritual communities. There are now countless stories of spiritual seekers who have been seriously harmed by spiritual teachers. During the course of my own meditation research, at least two well-known meditation teachers were accused of inappropriate sexual behaviour and sexual abuse. In such instances, spiritual bypassing may be used to abdicate an individual's responsibility for critical questioning or discernment regarding the behaviour of meditation teachers and the validity of their teachings. This form of justification and denial can manifest as excuse making—for example "the teacher was using the strategy of 'crazy wisdom'" or "enlightenment does not necessarily equate with morality." Another common strategy is victim blaming; ironically the capacity for judgment still seems to be effectively retained when it comes to blaming victims for the behaviour of abusive spiritual teachers or harmful practices. Victim blaming is often used to justify and explain the experiences of those who encounter meditation-related adverse effects, or those whose meditation experience does not fit the idealised meditation narrative. While it is likely that most meditation adverse effects involve an interaction between the practice of meditation and characteristics of the individual meditator, the issue is complex, and adverse experiences are not limited to people who have a history of, or proclivity towards, mental illness. Excuse making and victim blaming might provide some temporary relief from unwelcome feelings of cognitive dissonance, however ultimately these strategies allow systematic abuse and other adverse effects to continue unchallenged.

Although the term "spiritual bypassing" has been around since the 1980s, it seems that as a culture we still have not managed to outgrow this practice, particularly in context of meditation. Growing out of spiritual bypassing involves developing discernment regarding the myriad claims that are made about meditation—by teachers, organisations and the media. It also requires critical analysis regarding the many aspects of meditation practices; their stated aims, proposed mechanisms, history, cultural context, and limitations. Denying the dark side of meditation demonstrates lazy thinking and sometimes a basic lack of rationality that can result in harm to self and others.

The future

While the occurrence of meditation adverse effects may be rare (although at this stage the frequency of adverse effects is unknown), they do exist and are worthy of further scientific investigation. Future meditation research needs to investigate the full range of phenomenological experiences that occur for meditators, both positive and negative. An analysis of the available data suggests that not only are there adverse effects associated with meditation, but these adverse effects have been largely overlooked by the academic literature on meditation, and until very recently, largely unheard of in the mainstream media. Evidence from a variety of sources suggests that meditation may be associated with distressing and challenging side effects that in many cases appear similar to, but may be fundamentally different from, psychopathology.

An under-reporting of meditation adverse effects raises serious concerns regarding the possible risks associated with the use of meditation in both clinical and non-clinical populations. This issue is particularly relevant given the current popularity of secular meditation practices in a large variety of non-traditional settings including therapy, education and the workplace.

In particular, if meditation is going to be included as a component of, or alongside, psychotherapy, then we need a more spiritually literate psychology. Modern psychology and psychiatry are based on secular humanistic and scientific understandings of the human condition, and focus on the personal and the interpersonal. Eastern spiritual traditions, on the other hand, focus on the spiritual or *suprapersonal* (Welwood 2000), that which is above or beyond what is personal or transcends the merely personal. So far, no mainstream secular tradition has addressed all these aspects—personal, interpersonal and spiritual—within a single framework. Spirituality has achieved legitimacy in psychology to varying degrees. For example, there exist numerous research studies that emphasise its relevance and positive role in individuals' lives. However, at this stage, while religion and spirituality may have a place in psychological research, very little of this research has made its way into applied practice. Pargament et al. (2013) argue that this is due partly to a reluctance among psychologists to integrate religion and spirituality into the practice of psychology. To a certain extent this has been due to a desire to establish the discipline of psychology as a "hard science" and hence the subsequent avoidance of anything related to the supernatural or otherworldy. Interestingly, psychologists on the whole also tend to be less spiritual and religious compared to the general population. Pargament et al. (2013: 5) report:

> psychologists as a group are considerably more skeptical about the ontological validity of a sacred dimension than the general population in the United States. Although more than 90% of Americans report that they believe in God, only 24% of clinical and counseling psychologists do so. Perhaps as a result of their skepticism, psychologists tend to underestimate the significance of religion and spirituality in people's lives. Rather than treat these phenomena as legitimate and distinctive aspects of human functioning, they shift their focus to psychological, social, and physical processes that are

presumably more basic and more "real." There is, from this point of view, no need to focus on religion and spirituality in practice.

In fact, historically some of the leading figures in psychology have been openly hostile towards spirituality and religion:

> Some leading psychological figures, such as Freud and Skinner, go beyond skepticism to antagonism toward religion and spirituality, equating religious practices with pathology and discouraging psychologists from supporting this purportedly defensive way of life. Albert Ellis [...] founder of Rational Emotive Therapy, had this to say: "Obviously, the sane effective psychotherapist should not ... go along with the patient's religious orientation, for this is equivalent to trying to help them live successfully with their emotional illness" [... He did,] however, did soften his uniformly antagonistic position toward religion in his later writings (Pargament et al. 2013: 5).

The reluctance to acknowledge the relevance of spirituality and religion in applied psychology has resulted in a "spiritual illiteracy" in the discipline, or what some scholars have termed "spiritually avoidant care" (Vieten et al. 2013). In some cases, this lack of sensitivity and training regarding religious and spiritual issues may even result in religious and spiritual neglect in practice (Pargament et al. 2013). Ironically, despite modern Western psychology's history of skepticism, antagonism and spiritual illiteracy, psychologists are now commonly utilising meditation-based therapeutic techniques that derive from Eastern religious traditions. Up until now, practising psychologists may have been able to avoid being too explicit regarding the underlying religious and spiritual meanings of these techniques and practices (Pargament et al. 2013: 5). However, given the rapidly increasing popularity of meditation-based therapies and the recent research regarding meditation adverse effects, this approach seems unlikely to be able to continue. More careful consideration must be given to the origins of meditation practices, and their original stated aims.

Specifically, more research is needed regarding how meditation changes the psychological sense of self. A general argument presented in this book is that the traditional goal of meditation is the *realisation of non-self* whereas the goal of modern Western psychology and its related therapies is to *heal the self*. Whereas the Western meditation literature describes a beneficial shift in perspective that arises from meditation practice, the idea of non-self as defined by Buddhism (or true-self as defined by some schools of Hinduism) fits poorly into the contemporary Western therapeutic context, which focuses on the fulfilment of the individual's personal desires and the gratification of the psychological self. In fact, in the modern West, the notion of a private psychological self is so naturalised (and some would say revered) that any significant challenges to the reality of this self may pose problems. Additionally, because Western psychology does not currently have an explicit framework within which to explain meditation-related changes to self, these changes may be conflated with dissociative psychopathology, such as derealisation and depersonalisation. This is why some scholars have argued that there are instances where meditation is clearly contraindicated in psychotherapy, such as for those who already have an unstable sense of self or a predisposition to psychosis. Others have argued that meditation is entirely incompatible with Western therapy and should be kept in a separate realm of spiritual undertakings.

The problem lies partly with the fact that it is not entirely clear what Buddhism, Hinduism or Western psychology are referring to when they discuss the concept of the self. As Lindahl and Britton (2019) point out, the sense of self is understood in multiple ways. For example, there are a range of viewpoints regarding the Buddhist doctrine of *anattā* (non-self). Some scholars argue that it refers to a denial of the existence of "self as an enduring substance" (Gethin 1998: 145). Others suggest that non-self must include a "change in character" that includes an eradication of "personality belief" (*sakkāya-ditthi*) and the fundamental sense of the "ego" or "I am" (*asmimāna*) (e.g. Collins 1982). Similarly, the field of Western psychology contains multiple definitions and numerous theories regarding the self. While Britton and Lindahl (2009) have made an initial attempt to delineate six discrete categories of self-experience and understand how they relate to meditation, at this stage it is not entirely clear how contemplative explanations of self might map onto modern psychological definitions of self. This is an area that is ripe for future research. In the meantime, teachers of meditation and meditation-based therapies (both secular and non-secular) should be more specific and transparent regarding what changes in self their techniques are aiming for and why.

It is also important to note that a reduction in self-related processing is not always experienced as a positive thing. Lindahl and Britton (2019: 158) point out that given the popular therapeutic reading of Buddhist doctrines and practices, it is often assumed that a reduction in a sense of self will result in increased mental health or wellbeing. However, their study clearly demonstrates that this is not always the case. Their findings should not be particularly surprising given that changes in sense of self are also associated with almost all forms of psychopathology. Hence, delineating the multiple factors that make up the sense of self and understanding how various meditation practices impact these various self-aspects will be one of the challenges for meditation research going forward.

It should be clear by now that when it comes to meditation there are no clear boundaries between the secular and the religious. While many popular meditation practices are presented as secular, it is important to note that meditation derives from religion and is widely considered by many leading figures in the field as a deeply spiritual practice (e.g. Arat 2017; Hale 2018; Sharf 2015). There has been much debate regarding whether meditation can ever be successfully separated from its religious context and made "truly secular," with some critics of secular meditation noting that religious elements remain implicit even in clinical applications of meditation. When carefully scrutinised, the "East" and "West" divide is similarly artificial. For example, the idea that meditation techniques such as mindfulness and *vipassana* derive from a pure, ancient, unadulterated form of Buddhism is a myth. Globalisation, cross-border communication, and a myriad of other sociocultural factors have combined to influence the way that various forms of meditation have been, and continue to be, construed and practised throughout the world.

How do we successfully navigate the ambiguous secular/religious divide? How can secular meditation teachers productively engage with spiritual or religious traditions?

There are no quick and easy answers here. As meditation teacher Giovanni Dienstmann noted in one of our conversations, we are in a "live experiment:"

> For many centuries, meditation has always been a spiritual practice, taught by spiritual masters to spiritual aspirants. Human suffering in the form of anxiety, depression and stress was seen as an

entrance door to the spiritual path, a powerful fuel. The idea of teaching just the meditation mechanics—devoid of its ethical, soteriological and philosophical context—is a modern invention, a project of cultural colonialism.

This work in progress is built on the hypothesis that if we remove all spirituality from meditation, we will have a tool that will provide just enough self-transformation to be sought as a panacea for all evils, but not too much as to completely deconstruct one's identity, world view, and motivations in life. I'm not sure to what extent this outcome, if at all desirable, is possible.

Regardless of whether such a spiritually devoid version of meditation is even possible, transparency regarding the religious and spiritual origins, and original stated goals, of meditation allows potential practitioners to engage in genuine informed consent. My research did not consider the harm that may be done to those who feel deceived by practising a meditation technique that is marketed as secular but that has religious origins. However, a common theme that emerged from my correspondence with meditators was that they often started out by learning a secular meditation technique, such as a mindfulness-based modality, but then found themselves consulting Buddhist texts and teachers in order to troubleshoot their practice or seek further detail that their secular teacher was unable to provide. For some people, crossing over into Buddhist or Hindu territory does not pose a significant problem. For others, such as those who are deeply committed to another religious tradition, or consider themselves to be secular atheists, this is experienced as deception and can cause significant harm. As Aryeh Siegel (2018) notes in *Transcendental Deception*, "full disclosure" is a consumer expectation and people have a right to know about a meditation technique's origins, aims, and potential risks. As meditation moves from guru-centric transmission lineages to educational, professional and corporate settings, radical transparency and informed consent are essential.

To conclude, I hope it is clear that this book is not a criticism of meditation practices, practitioners, lineages, or teachers. There exist many happy meditation practitioners who may never encounter any of the issues mentioned in this book. Similarly, there are many sincere, experienced and technically proficient meditation teachers (both secular and non-secular) who are attempting to ethically and gracefully navigate these concerns. Rather, this book is an attempt at balance. Many factors have combined to create a popular, but inaccurate, portrayal of meditation as a simple, secular, science-aligned, and side-effect free solution for a variety of common problems. However, this is a radically simplified perspective that has led to meditation being viewed as a panacea and to adverse effects being overlooked and ignored. As Lazarus noted in 1984:

> Thus, my point is that meditation is no panacea—it is strongly indicated in some cases, mildly in others, and clearly contraindicated in others. The precise guidelines for these discriminations have yet to be worked out.[41]

Almost four decades later, we are still working it out.

---

[41] A.A. Lazarus, "Meditation: The Problems of Any Unimodal Technique," in *Meditation: Classic and Contemporary Perspectives*, eds. D.H. Shapiro, Jr and R.N. Walsh, 2009: 691.

REFERENCES

Adams, S. "Proof that Meditation CAN Grow Your Brain: In Just Eight Weeks It Can Improve Learning and Memory." *Daily Mail*. 2014. Online: https://www.dailymail.co.uk/health/article-2826953/Proof-meditation-grow-brain-just-eight-weeks-improve-learning-memory.html.

Aguirre, C. "Mindfulness and Mental Toughness." *Headspace*. 2015. Online: https://www.headspace.com/blog/2015/01/17/mindfulness-and-mental-toughness/.

Ahmed, S. "The Happiness Turn." *New Formations* vol. 63, no. 1 (2007): 7–14.

Aleksander, I. "Look Who's Meditating Now." *New York Times*. 18 March 2011. Online: https://www.nytimes.com/2011/03/20/fashion/20TM.html.

Altemeyer, B. "PERSPECTIVES: The Decline of Organized Religion in Western Civilization." *International Journal for the Psychology of Religion* vol. 14, no. 2 (2004): 77–89.

Amihai, I. and Kozhevnikov, M. "Arousal vs. Relaxation: A Comparison of the Neurophysiological and Cognitive Correlates of Vajrayana and Theravada Meditative Practices." *PLoS ONE* 9 no. 7 (2014).

Arat, A. "'What It Means to be Truly Human': The Postsecular Hack of Mindfulness." *Social Compass* vol. 64, no. 2 (2017): 167–179.

Assagioli, R. "Self-realization and Psychological Disturbances," in Grof and Grof (eds) *Spiritual Emergency: When Personal Transformation Becomes a Crisis*. New York, NY and Los Angeles, CA: Tarcher, 1989.

Awasthi, B. "Issues and Perspectives in Meditation Research: In Search for a Definition." *Frontiers in Psychology* 3 (2013): 1–9.
Bacher, P.G. "An Investigation into the Compatibility of Existential-Humanistic Psychotherapy and Buddhist Meditation." Educat. D, Boston University School of Education, MA (1981).
Baer, R. and Kuyken, W. "Is Mindfulness Safe?" *Oxford Mindfulness Centre*. October 2016. Online: http://oxfordmindfulness.org/news/is-mindfulness-safe/.
Barker, K.K. "Mindfulness Meditation: Do-it-Yourself Medicalization of Every Moment." *Social Science & Medicine* 106 (2014): 168–176.
Barnes, A. "The Happiest Man in the World?" *The Independent*. 21 January 2007. Online: https://www.independent.co.uk/news/uk/this-britain/the-happiest-man-in-the-world-433063.html.
Benedict, A.L., Mancini, L. and Grodin, M.A. "Struggling to Meditate: Contextualising Integrated Treatment of Traumatised Tibetan Refugee Monks." *Mental Health, Religion & Culture* vol. 12, no. 5 (2009): 485–499.
Benson, H. and Klipper, M.Z. *The Relaxation Response*. London, UK: Collins, 1976.
Berry, D.R., Cairo, A.H., Goodman, R.J., Quaglia, J.T., Green, J.D., Brown, K.W. "Mindfulness Increases Prosocial Responses toward Ostracized Strangers through Empathic Concern." *Journal of Experimental Psychology* vol. 147, no. 1 (2018): 93–112.
Bhikku Nanamoli. *Visuddhimagga: The Path of Purification*. Kandy, Sri Lanka: Buddhist Publication Society, 2011. Online: https://www.urbandharma.org/pdf1/PathofPurification2011.pdf.
Bhikshu Dharmamitra. *The Essentials of Buddhist Meditation: The Essentials for Practicing Calming-and-Insight & Dhyāna meditation—The Classic Śamathā-Vipaśyana Meditation Manual by the Great Tiantai Meditation Master & Exegete Śramaṇa Zhiyi*. Seattle, WA: Kalavinka Press, 2009.
Boals, G.F. "Toward a Cognitive Reconceptualization of Meditation." *The Journal of Transpersonal Psychology* vol. 10, no. 2 (1978): 143–182.
Bogart, G. "The Use of Meditation in Psychotherapy: A Review of the Literature." *American Journal of Psychotherapy* vol. 45, no. 3 (1991): 383–412.
Borup, J. "Branding Buddha—Mediatized and Commodified Buddhism as Cultural Narrative." *Journal of Global Buddhism* vol. 17 (2016): 41–55.
Bradwejn, J., Dowdall, M. and Iny, L. "Can East and West Meet in Psychoanalysis?" *American Journal of Psychiatry* 142 (1985): 1226–1228.
Brasington, L. "Leigh Brasington Interview." *Vimeo*, 2013. Online: https://vimeo.com/61893225.
Braun, E. *The Birth of Insight: Meditation, Modern Buddhism and the Burmese Monk Ledi Sayadaw*. Chicago, IL: The University of Chicago Press, 2013.
Braun, E. "The Insight Revolution." *Lion's Roar*. 5 July 2018. Online: https://www.lionsroar.com/the-insight-revolution/.

Brinson, S. "Hacking Your Brain Waves: A Guide to Wearable Meditation Headsets." *DIYGenius*. January 29, 2017. Online: https://www.diygenius.com/hacking-your-brain-waves/.
Britton, W. "The Dark Side of Dharma." *Buddhist Geeks*, 2011a. Online: https://art19.com/shows/buddhist-geeks/episodes/bb6cd056-ca75-42e0-bead-2d8d862aa46f.
Britton, W.B. "The Dark Night Project." *Buddhist Geeks*, 2011b. Online: https://art19.com/shows/buddhist-geeks/episodes/7c66e68d-ab9b-4a08-a21a-caa8d8a724f9.
Britton, W.B., Lindahl, J.R., Cahn, B.R., Davis, J.H. and Goldman, R.E. "Awakening is not a Metaphor: The Effects of Buddhist Meditation Practices on Basic Wakefulness." *Annals of the New York Academy of Sciences* 1307 (2013): 64–81.
Britton, W.B. and Lindahl, J.R. *Meditation*. Oxford Bibliographies Online, 2015.Online:http://www.oxfordbibliographies.com/view/document/obo-9780199828340/obo-9780199828340-0169.xml;jsessionid=F256F730A2B06D2EBEF5630E65C9DFB8.
Britton, W.B. and Sydnor, A. "Neurobiological Models of Meditation: Implications for Training Young People." In C. Willard and A. Salzmann (eds) *Teaching Mindfulness Skills to Kids and Teens*. New York, NY: Guilford Press, 2015.
Bronn, G. and McIlwain, D. "Assessing Spiritual Crises: Peeling Off Another Layer of a Seemingly Endless Onion." *Journal of Humanistic Psychology* vol. 55, no. 3 (2015): 346–382.
Brown, K.W., Ryan, R.M. and Creswell, J.D. "Mindfulness: Theoretical Foundations and Evidence for its Salutary Effects." *Psychological Inquiry* vol. 18, no. 4 (2007): 211–237.
Bulletproof Blog, website accessed October 2018. Online: https://blog.bulletproof.com/.
Bulletproof Staff, "The 7-Day Resilience Challenge: Build Mental Toughness for a Happier Life." *Bulletproof Blog*, 18 April 2017. Online: https://blog.bulletproof.com/7-day-resilience-challenge-build-mental-toughness-happier-life/.
Burrows, L. "Safeguarding Mindfulness Meditation for Vulnerable College Students." *Mindfulness* 7 (2016): 284–285.
Burrows, L. "'I Feel Proud We Are Moving Forward': Safeguarding Mindfulness for Vulnerable Student and Teacher Wellbeing in a Community College." *The Journal of Adult Protection* vol. 19, no. 1 (2017): 33–46.
Campbell, L. "'Compassion Meditation' Is the Best Type to Practise if Happiness Is Your Goal." *Huffington Post*. 2017. Online: https://www.huffingtonpost.com.au/2017/02/12/compassion-meditation-is-the-best-type-to-practise-if-happines_a_21712408/.

Carrette, J.R. and King, R. *Selling Spirituality: The Silent Takeover of Religion.* London and New York: Routledge, 2005.

Castillo, R.J. "Depersonalization and Meditation." *Psychiatry* 53 (1990): 158–168.

Cayton, A. (ed.) *Balanced Mind, Balanced Body: Anecdotes and Advice from Tibetan Buddhist Practitioners on Wind Disease.* Portland, OR: FPMT, 2016.

Cho, J. "How Meditation Increases Happiness." *Forbes*, 5 March 2016. Online: https://www.forbes.com/sites/jeenacho/2016/03/05/increase-happiness-and-sense-of-well-being-through-meditation/#18d4697a2adb.

Coe, J.H. "Musings on the Dark Night of the Soul: Insights from St. John of the Cross on a Developmental Spirituality." *Journal of Psychology and Theology* vol. 28, no. 4 (2000): 293–307.

Colgan, P. "OM THE FRONT PAGE: Rupert Murdoch Is Learning Transcendental Meditation." *Business Insider*. 2013. Online: https://www.businessinsider.com.au/om-the-front-page-rupert-murdoch-is-learning-transcendental-meditation-2013-4.

Collins, S. *Selfless Persons: Imagery and Thought in Theravāda Buddhism.* Cambridge, UK: Cambridge University Press, 1982.

Compson, J. "Meditation, Trauma and Suffering in Silence: Raising Questions about How Meditation is Taught and Practiced in Western Contexts in the Light of a Contemporary Trauma Resiliency Model." *Contemporary Buddhism* vol. 15, no. 2 (2014): 274–297.

Crouch, R. "The Bright Side of the Dark Night." *Aloha Dharma* website accessed July 2019. Online: https://alohadharma.com/2015/03/03/the-bright-side-of-the-dark-night/.

Culadasa (John Yates). *The Mind Illuminated: A Complete Meditation Guide.* Carlsbad, CA: Hay House, 2015.

Cusack, C.M. "The Western Reception of Buddhism: Celebrity and Popular Cultural Media as Agents of Familiarisation." *Journal for the Academic Study of Religion* vol. 24, no. 3 (2011): 297–316.

Davidson, R.J. and Begley, S. *The Emotional Life of Your Brain: How Its Unique Patterns Affect the Way You Think, Feel, and Live—and How You Can Change Them.* New York, NY: Hudson Street Press, 2012.

Davis, J.H. and Vago, D.R. "Can Enlightenment be Traced to Specific Neural Correlates, Cognition, or Behavior? No, and (a qualified) Yes." *Frontiers in Psychology* 4 (2013): 1–4.

Deikman, A.J. "Experimental Meditation." *Journal of Nervous and Mental Disease* 136 (1963): 329–343.

Deikman, A.J. "Implications of Experimentally Induced Contemplative Meditation." *Journal of Nervous and Mental Disease* 142 (1966): 101–116.

Diagnostic and Statistical Manual of Mental Disorders, Fifth Edition. Washington, DC: American Psychiatric Publishing, 2013.

Didonna, F. "Mindfulness and Obsessive-compulsive Disorder." In F. Didonna (ed) *Clinical Handbook of Mindfulness*. New York, NY: Springer Publishing, 2009.

Dissanayaka, N. "Is Mindfulness All It's Cracked Up To be?" *Huffington Post*. 2018. Online: https://www.huffingtonpost.co.uk/entry/the-rise-in-drug-related-mental-healthadmissions_uk_5ab9059ce4b0cde6b4f23cc0?guccounter=1&guce_referrer_us=aHR0cHM6Ly93d3cuZ29vZ2xlLmNvbNvbS8&guce_referrer_cs=KdhkPhdpIbRiRJ8ZUmnqRw

Dobkin, P.L., Irving, J.A. and Amar, S. "For Whom May Participation in a Mindfulness-Based Stress Reduction Program be Contraindicated?" *Mindfulness* 3 (2012): 44–50.

Dombrowski, D.A. *St. John of the Cross: An Appreciation*. Albany, NY: State University of New York Press, 1992.

Dorjee, D. "Defining Contemplative Science: The Metacognitive Self-Regulatory Capacity of the Mind, Context of Meditation Practice and Modes of Existential Awareness." *Frontiers in Psychology* 7 (2016): 1–15.

Drougge, P. "Notes Toward a Coming Backlash: Mindfulness as an Opiate of the Middle Classes." In R.E. Purser, D. Forbes and A. Burke (eds) *Handbook of Mindfulness: Culture, Context and Social Engagement*. Cham, Switzerland: Springer International Publishing, 2016.

Dryden, W. and Still, A. "Historical Aspects of Mindfulness and Self-acceptance in Psychotherapy." *Journal of Rational-Emotive and Cognitive-Behavior Therapy*, vol. 24, no. 1 (2006): 3–28.

Dubied, A. and Hanitzsch, T. "Studying Celebrity News." *Journalism* vol. 15, no. 2 (2014): 137–143.

Dulaney, M. "Looking for an Edge in Sport? How Mindfulness and Meditation can Boost Performance." *ABC News*. 2018. Online: https://www.abc.net.au/news/2018-09-15/mindfulness-meditation-sports-can-boost-performance/10215336.

Edelglass, W. "Buddhism, Happiness, and the Science of Meditation." In D.L. McMahan and E. Braun (eds) *Meditation, Buddhism, and Science*. New York, NY: Oxford University Press, 2017.

Ehara, N.R.M., Thera, S. and Thera, K. *Vimuttimagga: The Path of Freedom*. Kandy, Sri Lanka: Buddhist Publication Society, 1961. Online: http://urbandharma.org/pdf1/Path_of_Freedom_Vimuttimagga.pdf.

Eklöf, J. "Saving the World: Personalized Communication of Mindfulness Neuroscience." In R.E. Purser, D. Forbes and A. Burke (eds) *Handbook of Mindfulness: Culture, Context and Social Engagement*. Cham, Switzerland: Springer International Publishing, 2016.

Ellis, A. "The Place of Meditation in Cognitive-Behaviour Therapy and Rational-emotive Therapy." In D.H. Shapiro and R. N. Walsh (eds) *Meditation: Classic and Contemporary Perspectives*. New York, NY: Aldine Transaction, 2009.

Emerson, G.B., Warme, W.J., Wolf, F.M., Heckman, J.D., Brand, R.A. and Leopold, S.S. "Testing for the Presence of Positive-Outcome Bias in Peer Review: A Randomized Controlled Trial." *Archives of Internal Medicine* vol. 170, no. 21 (2010): 1934–1939.

Engler, J. "Therapeutic Aims in Psychotherapy and Buddhism." In K. Wilber, J. Engler and D. Brown (eds) *Transformations of Consciousness*. Boston, MA: Shambhala, 1986.

Engler, J. "Being Somebody and Being Nobody: A re-examination of the Understanding of Self in Psychoanalysis and Buddhism." In J.D. Safran (ed) *Psychoanalysis and Buddhism: An Unfolding Dialogue*. Somerville, MA: Wisdom Publications, 2003a.

Engler, J. "Reply: Can We Say What the Self 'Really' Is?" In J.D. Safran (ed) *Psychoanalysis and Buddhism: An Unfolding Dialogue*. Somerville, MA: Wisdom Publications, 2003b.

Engler, J. "Promises and Perils of the Spiritual Path." In M. Unno (ed) *Buddhism and Psychotherapy: Across Cultures*. Boston: Wisdom Publications, 2006.

Epstein, M. *Thoughts Without a Thinker*. New York, NY: Basic Books, 1995.

Epstein, M. *Psychotherapy Without the Self: A Buddhist Perspective*. New Haven, CT: Yale University Press, 2007.

Epstein, M. and Rapgay, L. "Mind, Disease, and Health in Tibetan Medicine." In A. A. Sheikh and K. S. Sheikh (eds) *Eastern and Western Approaches to Healing: Ancient Wisdom and Modern Knowledge*. New York, NY: Wiley, 1989.

Fallot, R.D. "Spirituality and Religion in Psychiatric Rehabilitation and Recovery from Mental Illness." *International Review of Psychiatry* vol. 13, no. 2 (2001): 110–116.

Farias, M. and Wikholm, C. *The Buddha Pill: Can Meditation Change You?* London: Watkins, 2015.

Farias, M. and Wikholm, C. "What Mindfulness Gurus Won't Tell You: Meditation Has a Dark Side." *Spectator Health*, 11 March 2016. Online: https://health.spectator.co.uk/what-mindfulness-gurus-dont-tell-you-meditation-has-a-dark-side/.

Feuerstein, G. "Yogic Meditation." In J. Shear (ed) *The Experience of Meditation: Experts Introduce the Major Traditions*. St. Paul, MN: Paragon House, 2006.

Feuerstein, G. *The Yoga Tradition: Its History, Literature, Philosophy and Practice*. Chino Valley, Arizona: Hohm Press, 2008.

Fields, R. *How the Swans Came to the Lake: A Narrative History of Buddhism in America.* Boulder, Colorado: Shambhala Publications, 1992.
Foster, D. "Is Mindfulness Making Us Ill?" *The Guardian*, 23 January 2016. Online: https://www.theguardian.com/lifeandstyle/2016/jan/23/is-mindfulness-making-us-ill.
French, A.P., Schmid, A.C. and Ingalls, E. "Transcendental Meditation, Altered Reality Testing, and Behavioral Change: A Case Report." *The Journal of Nervous and Mental Disease* vol. 161, no. 1 (1975): 55–58.
Fromm, E., Suzuki, D.T. and de Martino, R. *Psychoanalysis and Zen Buddhism.* New York, NY: Harper, [1974] 1993.
Fulton, C.L. "Self-Compassion as a Mediator of Mindfulness and Compassion for Others." *Counseling and Values* vol. 63, no. 1 (2018): 45–56.
Gander, K. "Katy Perry Says She Treats Her Anxiety With Meditation, Not Prescription Drugs." *Newsweek*, 28 April 2018. Online: http://www.newsweek.com/katy-perry-904893.
Gelles, D. "The Hidden Price of Mindfulness." *New York Times*, March 19, 2016.
Germer, C.K. "Teaching Mindfulness in Therapy." In C. K. Germer, R.D. Siegal and P.R. Fulton (eds) *Mindfulness and Psychotherapy.* New York, NY: Guilford Publications, 2005.
Gethin, R. *The Foundations of Buddhism.* Oxford, NY: Oxford University Press, 1998.
Gleig, A. *American Dharma: Buddhism Beyond Modernity.* New Haven, CT: Yale University Press, 2019.
Gleig, A. "From Theravada to Tantra: The Making of an American Tantric Buddhism?" *Contemporary Buddhism* vol. 14, no. 2 (2013): 221–238.
Gleig, A. "Wedding the Personal and Impersonal in West Coast Vipassana: A Dialogical Encounter between Buddhism and Psychotherapy." *Journal of Global Buddhism* 13 (2012): 129–146.
Goenka, S.N. *Buddha: The Super-Scientist of Peace.* Keynote address at the United Nations on May 28, 2002. Online: https://store.pariyatti.org/Buddha-The-Super-scientist-of-Peace-br-spanVipassanaspan_p_4714.html.
Goldberg, P. *American Veda: From Emerson and the Beatles to Yoga and Meditation How Indian Spirituality Changed the West.* New York, NY: Three Rivers Press, 2010.
Goleman, D. "Meditation as Meta-therapy: Hypotheses Toward a Proposed Fifth State of Consciousness." *Journal of Transpersonal Psychology* 3 (1971): 1–26.
Goleman, D. *The Meditative Mind.* New York, NY: Tarcher, 1988.
Goyal, M., Singh, S., Sibinga, E.M.S., Gould, N.F., Rowland-Seymour, A., Sharma, R., Berger, Z., Sleicher, D., Maron, D.D., Shihab, H.M.,

Ranasinghe, P.D., Linn, S., Saha, S., Bass, E.B. and Haythornthwaite, J.A. "Meditation Programs for Psychological Stress and Well-being: A Systematic Review and Meta-Analysis." *JAMA Internal Medicine* vol. 174, no. 3 (2014): 357–368.

Grabovac, A.D., Lau, M.A. and Willett, B.R. "Mechanisms of Mindfulness: A Buddhist Psychological Model." *Mindfulness* 2 (2011): 154–166.

Grabovac, A. "The Stages of Insight: Clinical Relevance for Mindfulness-based Interventions." *Mindfulness* 6 (2015): 1–13.

Greene, E. "Healing Sickness Caused by Meditation: 'The Enveloping Butter Contemplation' from the Secret Essential Methods for Curing Meditation Sickness." In C.P. Salguero (ed) *Buddhism and Medicine: An Anthology of Premodern Sources*. New York, NY: Columbia University Press, 2017.

Gregoire, C. "Why 2014 Will Be the Year of Mindful Living." *Huffington Post*, March 1, 2014. Online: http://www.huffingtonpost.com.au/entry/will-2014-be-the-year-of-_0_n_4523975.

Greyson, B. "The Physio-Kundalini Syndrome and Mental Illness." *The Journal of Transpersonal Psychology* vol. 25, no. 1 (1993): 43–58.

Grof, S. and Grof, C. *Spiritual Emergency: When Personal Transformation Becomes a Crisis*. New York and Los Angeles: Tarcher, 1989.

Gunther Brown, C. *The Healing Gods: Complementary and Alternative Medicine in Christian America*. New York, NY: Oxford University Press, 2013.

Gunther Brown, C. "Can 'Secular' Mindfulness Be Separated from Religion?" In R.E. Purser, D. Forbes and A. Burke (eds) *Handbook of Mindfulness: Culture, Context and Social Engagement*. Cham, Switzerland: Springer International Publishing, 2016.

Habermas, J. "Religion in the Public Sphere." *European Journal of Philosophy* vol. 14, no. 1 (2006): 1–25.

Hale, M. "Perfectly Present: Mindfulness Curriculum as Implicit Religion." *Implicit Religion* vol. 20, no. 4 (2018): 335–365.

Harris, D. *10% Happier* podcast #79: W.B. Britton and J.R. Lindahl "Does Meditation Have a Dark Side?" 2017. Online: https://player.fm/series/10-happier-with-dan-harris/79-willoughby-britton-jared-lindahl-does-meditation-have-a-dark-side.

Harvey, M. *Celebrity Influence: Politics, Persuasion, and Issue-Based Advocacy*. Lawrence, Kansas: University Press of Kansas, 2017.

Hayes, S.C. and Shenk, C. "Operationalizing Mindfulness without Unnecessary Attachments." *Clinical Psychology: Science and Practice* vol. 11, no. 3 (2004): 249–254.

Heuman, L. "Don't Believe the Hype: An Interview with Catherine Kerr." *Tricycle*, 1 October 2014. Online: https://tricycle.org/trikedaily/dont-believe-hype/.

Hergovich, A., Schott, R. and Burger, C. "Biased Evaluation of Abstracts Depending on Topic and Conclusion: Further Evidence of a Confirmation Bias within Scientific Psychology." *Current Psychology* vol. 29, no. 3 (2010): 188–209.

Hickey, W.S. "Mind Cure, Meditation, and Medicine: Hidden Histories of Mental Healing in the United States." Unpublished PhD Dissertation. Duke University, 2008.

Hoffman, S.J. and Tan, C. "Biological, Psychological and Social Processes that Explain Celebrities' Influence on Patients' Health-related Behaviours." *Archives of Public Health* 72 (2015): 1–11.

Humes, C.A. "The Transcendental Meditation Organization and its Encounter with Science." In J.R. Lewis and O. Hammer (eds) *Handbook of Religion and the Authority of Science*. Leiden, The Netherlands: Brill, 2010.

Hunter, K.M. "'There Was This One Guy . . .': The Uses of Anecdotes in Medicine." *Perspectives in Biology and Medicine* vol. 29, no. 4 (1986): 619–630.

Huntington Jr., C.W. "Are You Looking to Buddhism When You Should Be Looking to Therapy?" *Tricycle*, Spring 2018. Online: https://tricycle.org/magazine/buddhism-and-psychotherapy/.

Hyland, T. "McDonaldizing Spirituality: Mindfulness, Education, and Consumerism." *Journal of Transformative Education* vol. 15, no. 4 (2017): 334–356.

Ingram, D.M. *Mastering the Core Teachings of the Buddha: An Unusually Hardcore Dharma Book*. London, UK: Aeon Books Ltd, 2018.

Ivtzan, I. "Dangers of Meditation." *Psychology Today*, 11 March 2016. Online: https://www.psychologytoday.com/intl/blog/mindfulness-wellbeing/201603/dangers-meditation.

James, W. *The Varieties of Religious Experience*. New York, NY: Barnes & Noble, 2004 [1902].

Jones, R.H. *Piercing the Veil: Comparing Science and Mysticism as Ways of Knowing Reality*. New York, NY: Jackson Square Books, 2010.

Jung, C.G. *The Collected Works. Volumes I—XX*. Edited by Sir Herbert Read. New York, NY: Routledge, 2014.

Kabat-Zinn, J. *Full Catastrophe Living: Using the Wisdom of Your Body and Mind to Face Stress, Pain and Illness*. New York, NY: Delacorte Press, 1990.

Kabat-Zinn, J. "Mindfulness-based Interventions in Context: Past, Present, and Future." *Clinical Psychology: Science and Practice* vol. 10, no. 2 (2003): 144–156.

Kabat-Zinn, J. "Some Reflections on the Origins of MBSR, Skilful Means, and the Trouble with Maps." *Contemporary Buddhism* vol. 12, no. 1 (2011): 281–306.

Kabat-Zinn, J. "Lovingkindness Meditation." *Mindfulness* vol. 8, no. 4 (2017): 1117–1121.

Kabat-Zinn, *Wherever You Go, There You Are*. New York, NY: Hyperion, 1994.

Kachan, D., Olano, H., Tannenbaum, S.L., Annane, D.W., Mehta, A., Arheart, K.L., Fleming, L.E., Yang, X., Mcclure, L.A. and Lee, D.J. "Prevalence of Mindfulness Practices in the US Workforce: National Health Interview Survey." *Preventing Chronic Disease* 14 (2017).

Kaplan, D. "10-Minute Mindfulness Meditation to Reduce Stress." *Forbes*. 2017. Online: https://www.forbes.com/sites/dinakaplan/2017/03/24/10-minute-mindfulness-meditation-to-reduce-stress/#1562be46d02e.

Kapleau, P. *The Three Pillars of Zen: Teaching, Practice, and Enlightenment*. New York, NY: Anchor Books, 2000.

Kelsey-Sugg, A. and Zajac, B. "'Mental Hygiene' Could Improve Your Life—But Does It Improve Your Health?" ABC News. 2018. Online: https://www.abc.net.au/news/2018-10-17/dan-siegel-on-distractions-and-mental-health-hygiene/10343984.

Kennedy, R.B. "Self-induced Depersonalisation Syndrome." *American Journal of Psychiatry* vol. 133, no. 11 (1976): 1326–1328.

Klatt, M., Steinberg. B. and Duchemin, A.M. "Mindfulness in Motion (MIM): An Onsite Mindfulness Based Intervention (MBI) for Chronically High Stress Work Environments to Increase Resiliency and Work Engagement." *Journal of Visualized Experiments* 101 (2015): 1–11.

Klostermaier, K.K. *A Survey of Hinduism* (3rd Ed.). Albany, NY: State University of New York Press, 2007.

Knapton, S. "Grow Your Own Happiness: How Meditation Physically Changes the Brain." *The Telegraph*, 20 November 2015. Online: https://www.telegraph.co.uk/news/science/science-news/12008698/Grow-your-own-happiness-how-meditation-physically-changes-the-brain.html.

Kornfield, J.M. "The Psychology of Mindfulness Meditation." Unpublished PhD Dissertation, Saybrook Institute, 1977.

Kornfield, J. "Intensive Insight Meditation: A Phenomenological Study." *The Journal of Transpersonal Psychology* vol. 11, no. 1 (1979): 41–58.

Kornfield, J. "Meditation and Psychotherapy: A Plea for Integration." *Inquiring Mind* vol. 5, no. 1 (1988).

Kornfield, J. "Obstacles and Vicissitudes in Spiritual Practice." in S. Grof and C. Grof (eds) *Spiritual Emergency: When Personal Transformation Becomes a Crisis*. New York and Los Angeles: Tarcher, 1989.

Kornfield, J. *A Path With Heart*. New York, NY: Bantam Books, 1993a.

Kornfield, J. "Even the Best Meditators Have Old Wounds to Heal: Combining Meditation and Psychotherapy." In R.N. Walsh and F. Vaughan (eds)

Paths Beyond Ego: The Transpersonal Vision. New York, NY: Tarcher Penguin, 1993b.

Kornfield, J. *After the Ecstasy, the Laundry: How the Heart Grows Wise on the Spiritual Path.* New York, NY: Bantam Books, 2000.

Kozhevnikov, M., Louchakova, O., Josipovic, Z. and Motes, M.A. "The Enhancement of Visuospatial Processing Efficiency Through Buddhist Deity Meditation." *Psychological Science* vol. 20, no. 5 (2009): 645–653.

Kripal, J.J. *Esalen: America and the Religion of no Religion.* Chicago, IL: University of Chicago Press, 2007.

Krishna, G. *The Awakening of Kundalini.* Ontario: Institute for Consciousness Research, 2001.

Kuijpers, H., van der Heijden, F., Tuinier, S. and Verhoeven, W. "Meditation-Induced Psychosis." *Psychopathology* 40 (2007): 461–464.

Kutz, I., Borysenko, J.Z. and Benson, H. "Meditation and Psychotherapy: A Rationale for the Integration of Dynamic Psychotherapy, the Relaxation Response, and Mindfulness Meditation." *American Journal of Psychiatry* vol. 142, no. 1 (1985): 1–8.

Lalich, J. and McLaren, K. *Escaping Utopia: Growing Up in a Cult, Getting Out, and Starting Over.* London, UK: Taylor and Francis, 2017.

Lauder, J. "'Nothing Bad Can Happen': What Happens When Meditation Goes Wrong." *Triple J HACK*, 12 July 2018. Online: http://www.abc.net.au/triplej/programs/hack/meditation-negatives/9987132.

Lauricella, S. "The Ancient-Turned-New Concept of 'Spiritual Hygiene': An Investigation of Media Coverage of Meditation from 1979 to 2014." *Journal of Religion and Health* vol. 55, no. 5 (2014): 1748–1762.

Lazar, S.W., Kerr, C.E., Wasserman, R.H., Gray, J.R., Greve, D.N., Treadway, M.T., Mcgarvey, M., Quinn, B.T., Dusek, J.A., Benson, H.I., Rauch, S.L., Moore, C.I., Fischl, B.I. "Meditation Experience is Associated with Increased Cortical Thickness." *Neuroreport* vol. 16, no. 17 (2005): 1893–1897.

Lazarus, A. "Psychiatric Problems Precipitated by Transcendental Meditation." *Psychological Reports* 39 (1976): 601–602.

Lazarus, A.A. and Mayne, T.J. "Relaxation: Some Limitations, Side Effects, and Proposed Solutions." *Psychotherapy* vol. 27, no. 2 (1990): 261–266.

Ledi, S. *The Manual of Dhamma.* Igatpuri, India: VRI, 1999.

Lindahl, J.R., Fisher, N.E., Cooper, D.J., Rosen, R.K. and Britton, W.B. "The Varieties of Contemplative Experience: A Mixed-methods Study of Meditation-related Challenges in Western Buddhists." *PLoS ONE* vol. 12, no. 5 (2017).

Lindahl, J. R., and Britton, W.B. "'I Have This Feeling of Not Really Being Here': Buddhist Meditation and Changes in Sense of Self." *Journal of Consciousness Studies* vol. 26, no. 7–8 (2019): 157–83.

Lomas, T., Cartwright, T., Edginton, T. and Ridge, D. "A Qualitative Analysis of Experiential Challenges Associated with Meditation Practice." *Mindfulness* vol. 6, no. 4 (2015): 848–860.

Lopez Jr, D.S. *Buddhism and Science: A Guide for the Perplexed*. London: University of Chicago Press, 2008.

Luberto, C., Shinday, N., Song, R., Philpotts, L., Park, E., Fricchione, G. and Yeh, G. "A Systematic Review and Meta-Analysis of the Effects of Meditation on Empathy, Compassion, and Prosocial Behaviors." *Mindfulness* vol. 9, no. 3 (2018): 708–724.

Lukoff, D., Lu, F. and Turner, R. "From Spiritual Emergency to Spiritual Problem: The Transpersonal Roots of the New DSM-IV Category." *Journal of Humanistic Psychology* vol. 38, no. 2 (1998): 21–50.

Lukoff, D., Provenzano, R., Lu, F. and Turner, R. "Religious and Spiritual Case Reports on MEDLINE: A Systematic Analysis of Records from 1980 to 1996." *Alternative Therapies in Health and Medicine* vol. 5, no. 1 (1999): 64–70.

Lustyk, M.K.B., Chawla, N., Nolan, R.S. and Marlatt, A.G. "Mindfulness Meditation Research: Issues of Participant Screening, Safety Procedures, and Researcher Training." *ADVANCES* vol. 24, no. 1 (2009): 20–30.

Lutkajtis, A. "The Dark Side of Dharma: Why Have Adverse Effects of Meditation Been Ignored in Contemporary Western Secular Contexts?" *Journal for the Academic Study of Religion* vol. 31, no. 2 (2019): 192–217.

Lutz, A., Slagter, H.A., Dunne, J.D. and Davidson, R.J. "Attention Regulation and Monitoring in Meditation." *Trends in Cognitive Sciences* 12 (2008): 163–169.

Lynch, G., Mitchell, J.P and Strhan. A. *Religion, Media and Culture: A Reader*. Routledge, London and New York, 2012.

Mahan, J.H. *Media, Religion and Culture: An Introduction*. Routledge, New York, 2014.

Maslow, A. *The Farther Reaches of Human Nature*. New York, NY: Viking, 1971.

Masters, R.A. *Spiritual Bypassing: When Spiritualty Disconnects Us From What Really Matters*. Berkeley, CA: North Atlantic Books, 2010.

McAdams, D.P. and McLean, K.C. Narrative Identity. *Current Directions in Psychological Science*, vol. 22, no. 3 (2013): 233–238.

McMahan, D.L. *The Making of Buddhist Modernism*. New York, NY: Oxford University Press, 2008.

McMahan, D.L. and Braun, E. *Meditation, Buddhism and Science*. New York, NY: Oxford University Press, 2017.

Michaelson, J. "What If Meditation Isn't Good for You?" *Daily Beast*, November 1, 2014. Online: http://www.thedailybeast.com/articles/2014/11/01/what-if-meditation-isn-t-good-for-you.html.

Mitchell, S. "The Tranquil Meditator: Representing Buddhism and Buddhists in US Popular Media." *Religion Compass* vol. 8, no. 3 (2014): 81–89.

Murphy, M. and Donovan, S. *The Physical and Psychological Effects of Meditation: A Review of Contemporary Research with a Comprehensive Bibliography 1931–1996.* CA: Institute of Noetic Sciences, 1999.

Narada Maha Thera. *A Manual of Abhidhamma.* Kuala Lumpur, Malaysia: Buddhist Missionary Society, 1987. Online: http://www.buddhanet.net/pdf_file/abhidhamma.pdf.

Nelson, L.W. "Chan (Zen) Sickness and the Master's Role in its Diagnosis, Treatment, and Prevention." Unpublished PhD dissertation. California Institute of Integral Studies, 2012.

Newman, M.G., Lafreniere, L.S. and Jacobson, N.C. "Relaxation-induced Anxiety: Effects of Peak and Trajectories of Change on Treatment Outcome for Generalised Anxiety Disorder." *Psychotherapy Research* vol. 28, no. 4 (2018): 616–629.

Nickerson, R.S. "Confirmation Bias: A Ubiquitous Phenomenon in Many Guises." *Review of General Psychology* vol. 2, no. 2 (1998): 175–220.

Nishijima. G.W. and Warner, B. *Nagarjuna's Mulamadhyamakakarika: Fundamental Wisdom of the Middle Way.* Rhinebeck, NY: Monkfish, 2011.

Ohanian, R. "The Impact of Celebrity Spokespersons' Perceived Image on Consumers' Intention to Purchase." *Journal of Advertising Research* vol. 31, no. 1 (1991): 46–54.

Oliver, P. *Hinduism and the 1960s: The Rise of a Counter-Culture.* London: Bloomsbury, 2014.

Otis, L.S. "Adverse Effects of Transcendental Meditation." In D.H. Shapiro and R.N. Walsh (eds) *Meditation: Classic and Contemporary Perspectives.* New York, NY: Aldine Transaction, 2009 [1984]: 201–208.

Ozawa-de Silva, B. "Contemplative Science and Secular Ethics." *Religions* vol. 7, no. 8 (2016): 1–20.

Paine, J. *Re-Enchantment: Tibetan Buddhism Comes to the West.* New York, NY: Norton, 2004.

Paranjpe, A.C. "Indian Psychology and the International Context." *Psychology and Developing Societies* vol. 23, no. 1 (2011): 1–26.

Pargament, K., Mahoney, A., Shafranske, E.P., Exline, J.J. and Jones, J.W. "From Research to Practice: Toward an Applied Psychology of Religion and Spirituality." In *American Psychological Association Handbook of Psychology, Religion and Spirituality (Vol 2): An Applied Psychology of Religion and Spirituality.* PsycBOOKS (American Psychological Association), 2013.

Parsons, W.B. "Psychoanalysis Meets Buddhism: The Development of a Dialogue." In J. Belzen (ed) *Changing the Scientific Study of Religion: Beyond Freud?* New York and London: Springer, 2009.

Partridge, C. *The Re-enchantment of the West: Alternative Spiritualities, Sacralization, Popular Culture and Occulture.* London, UK: T&T Clark International, 2004.

Paterniti, M. "The World's Happiest Man Wishes You Wouldn't Call Him That." *GQ*, 13 October 2016. Online: https://www.gq.com/story/happiest-man-in-the-world-matthieu-ricard.

Payne, R.K. "Mindfulness and the Moral Imperative for the Self to Improve the Self." In R.E. Purser, D. Forbes and A. Burke (eds) *Handbook of Mindfulness: Culture, Context and Social Engagement.* Cham, Switzerland: Springer International Publishing, 2016.

Perls, F. *Gestalt Therapy Verbatim.* Lafayette, CA: Real People Press, 1969.

Pickert, K. "The Mindful Revolution." *TIME Magazine*, February 3, 2014. Online: http://content.time.com/time/subscriber/article/0,33009,2163560,00.html.

Pflugshaupt, A. "Mental Hygiene—Madison Researcher Uses Modern Neuroscience to Study Kindness, Compassion & Happiness." *nbc15.* 2018. Online: https://www.nbc15.com/content/news/Mental-Hygiene--500882441.html.

Prebish, C.S. *Luminous Passage: The Practice and Study of Buddhism in America.* Berkeley, University of California Press, 1999.

Pringle, G. "Naomi Watts on 'While We're Young', Her Roots and Being a Mum." *The Independent*, 30 March 2015. Online: https://www.independent.co.uk/arts-entertainment/films/features/naomi-watts-on-while-were-young-her-roots-and-being-a-mum-10144541.html.

Pritchard, S.M. "Mindfulness and Beyond: A Qualitative Study of Advanced Mahasi Meditators' Experience." Unpublished PhD dissertation. Fielding Graduate University, 2016.

Purser, R. "The Myth of the Present Moment." *Mindfulness* vol. 6, no. 3 (2015): 680–686.

Purser, R.E. *McMindfulness: How Mindfulness Became the New Capitalist Spirituality.* London, UK: Repeater Books, 2019.

Raghavendra, B.R. and Singh, P. "Immediate Effect of Yogic Visual Concentration on Cognitive Performance." *Journal of Traditional and Complementary Medicine* 6 (2016): 34–36.

Rao, K.R. *Cognitive Anomalies, Consciousness and Yoga.* New Delhi, India: Matrix, 2010.

Raskin, N. and Rogers, C. "Person-centered Therapy." In R. Corsini and D. Wedding (eds) *Current Psychotherapies.* Itasca, IL: F.E. Peacock, 1995.

Remski, M.D. *Practice and All is Coming: Abuse, Cult Dynamics, and Healing in Yoga and Beyond.* Embodied Wisdom Publishing, 2019.

Richmond, L. "What the Teachers Say About Emptiness: Removing 'Lazy Nihilism' from Shunyata—or 'How Deep the Rabbit Hole Goes' and

'How Big is the Moon?'" *Buddha Weekly*. Online: https://buddhaweekly.com/what-the-teachers-say-about-emptiness-removing-lazy-nihilism-from-shunyata-or-how-deep-the-rabbit-hole-goes-and-how-big-is-the-moon/.

Rieff, P. *The Triumph of the Therapeutic: Uses of Faith After Freud*. Wilmington, DE: ISI Books, 2006.

Rocha, T. "The Dark Knight of the Soul." *The Atlantic*. 25 June 2014. Online. https://www.theatlantic.com/health/archive/2014/06/the-dark-knight-of-the-souls/372766/.

Rosch, E. "Is Wisdom in the Brain?" *Psychological Science* vol. 10, no. 3 (1999): 222–224.

Rosch, E. "How to Catch James' Mystic Germ: Religious Experience, Buddhist Meditation, and Psychology." *Journal of Consciousness Studies* vol. 9, no. 9–10 (2002): 37–56.

Rosenthal, N.E. "How Meditation Changed Hugh Jackman's Life." *Oprah*. 26 May 2016. Online: http://www.oprah.com/inspiration/how-meditation-changed-hugh-jackmans-life.

Rosenthal, R. "The File Drawer Problem and Tolerance for Null Results." *Psychological Bulletin* vol. 86, no. 3 (1979): 638–641.

Routledge, C. and Arndt, J. "Time and Terror: Managing Temporal Consciousness and the Awareness of Mortality." In A. Strathman & J. Joireman (eds) *Understanding Behavior in the Context of Time: Theory, Research, and Application*. Lawrence Erlbaum Associates Publishers, 2005.

Safran, J.D. (ed). *Psychoanalysis and Buddhism: An Unfolding Dialogue*. Boston, MA: Wisdom Publications, 2003.

Salguero, C.P. *Buddhism and Medicine: An Anthology of Premodern Sources*. New York, NY: Columbia University Press, 2017.

Samuel, G. "Unbalanced Flows in the Subtle Body: Tibetan Understandings of Psychiatric Illness and How to Deal with It." *Journal of Religion and Health* vol. 58, no. 3 (2019): 770–794.

Samuel, G. "The Contemporary Mindfulness Movement and the Question of Non-self." *Transcultural Psychiatry* vol. 52, no. 4 (2015): 485–500.

Sannella, L. "Kundalini: Classical and Clinical." In S. Grof and C. Grof (eds) *Spiritual Emergency: When Personal Transformation Becomes a Crisis*. New York and Los Angeles: Tarcher, 1989.

Santorelli, S. *Mindfulness-Based Stress Reduction (MBSR): Standards of Practice*. Worcester, MA: Center for Mindfulness in Medicine, Health Care, and Society, University of Massachusetts Medical School, 2014.

Schwartz, S.Y. "The Science Behind Why Meditation Makes You So Much Happier." *MindBodyGreen*. 2018. Online: https://www.mindbodygreen.com/0-29583/the-science-behind-why-meditation-makes-you-so-much-happier.html.

Sedikides, C., Wildschut, T. and Baden, D. "Nostalgia: Conceptual Issues and Existential Functions." In J. Greenberg, S. L. Koole, and T. Pyszczynski (eds) *Handbook of Experimental Existential Psychology*. Guilford Press, 2004.

Sedlmeier, P., Eberth, J., Schwarz, M., Zimmermann, D., Haarig, F., Jaeger, S. and Kunze, S. "The Psychological Effects of Meditation: A Meta-analysis." *Psychological Bulletin* vol. 138, no. 6 (2012): 1139–1171.

Sedlmeier, P. and Srinivas, K. "How do Theories of Cognition and Consciousness in Ancient Indian Thought Systems Relate to Current Western Theorizing and Research?" *Frontiers in Psychology* 7 (2016): 1–17.

Seppälä, E. M. "20 Scientific Reasons to Start Meditating Today." *Psychology Today*. 2013. Online: https://www.psychologytoday.com/au/blog/feeling-it/201309/20-scientific-reasons-start-meditating-today.

Seiden, D.Y. and Lam, K. "From Moses and Monotheism to Buddha and Behaviorism: Cognitive Behavior Therapy's Transpersonal Crisis." *Journal of Transpersonal Psychology* vol. 42, no. 1 (2010): 89–113.

Shapiro, D. "Adverse Effects of Meditation: A Preliminary Investigation of Long-term Meditators." *International Journal of Psychosomatics* 39 (1992): 62–67.

Shapiro, D.H. "Classic Perspectives of Meditation: Toward an Empirical Understanding of Meditation as an Altered State of Consciousness." In D.H. Shapiro and R.N. Walsh (eds) *Meditation: Classic and Contemporary Perspectives*. New York, NY: Aldine Transaction, 2009 [1984].

Shapiro, S.L., Carlson, L.E., Astin, J.A. and Freedman, B. "Mechanisms of Mindfulness." *Journal of Clinical Psychology* vol. 62, no. 3 (2006): 373–386.

Shapiro, D.H. and Walsh, R.N. (eds). *Meditation: Classic and Contemporary Perspectives*. New York, NY: Aldine Transaction, 2009.

Sharf, R. "Buddhist Modernism and the Rhetoric of Meditative Experience." *Numen* vol. 42, no. 3 (1995): 228–283.

Sharf, R.H. "Is Mindfulness Buddhist? (and Why it Matters)." *Transcultural Psychiatry* vol. 52, no. 4 (2015): 470–484.

Shear, J. *The Experience of Meditation: Experts Introduce the Major Traditions*. St. Paul, MN: Paragon House, 2006.

Shinzen Young, website online: https://www.shinzen.org/.

Shunsky, S. "The Beatles and the Guru," *USA Today*. January 2018. Online: http://www.divinerevelation.org/USATodayMagBeatles.pdf.

Siderits, M and Katsura, S. *Nagarjuna's Middle Way: The Mulamadhyamakakarika*. Boston, MA: Wisdom Publications, 2013.

Siegel, A. *Transcendental Deception: Behind the TM Curtain—Bogus Science, Hidden Agendas, and David Lynch's Campaign to Push a Million Public School Kids Into Transcendental Meditation While Falsely Claiming it is Not a Religion*. Janreg Press, 2018.

Singleton, M. *Yoga Body: The Origins of Modern Posture Practice*. New York, Oxford: Oxford University Press, 2010.
Smith, J.C. "Meditation as Psychotherapy: A Review of the Literature." *Psychological Bulletin* vol. 82, no. 4 (1975): 558–564.
Sperry, L. "Spiritually Sensitive Psychotherapy: An Impending Paradigm Shift in Theory and Practice." In L. Miller (ed) *The Oxford Handbook of Psychology and Spirituality*. New York, NY: Oxford University Press, 2012.
Spirit Rock, website online: https://www.spiritrock.org/about.
Stahl, A. "How to Practice Mindfulness at Work." *Forbes*. September 14, 2017. Online: https://www.forbes.com/sites/ashleystahl/2017/09/14/how-to-practice-mindfulness-at-work/#5656b674d57b.
Stanley, S., Purser, R.E. and Singh, N.N. (eds). *Handbook of Ethical Foundations of Mindfulness*. Cham, Switzerland: Springer International Publishing, 2018.
Stevens, R. and Rusby, J. "'The Angelina Effect': The Effect of High Profile Media Coverage on Referrals to a Family History Breast Clinic." *European Journal of Surgical Oncology* vol. 40, no. 5 (2014): 643–643.
Suler, J. *Contemporary Psychoanalysis and Eastern Thought*. Albany, NY: State University Press of New York, 1993.
Sun, J. "Mindfulness in Context: A Historical Discourse Analysis." *Contemporary Buddhism* vol. 5, no. 2 (2014): 394–415.
Swami, J. "Meditation on the Self and Superconsciousness." *International Journal of Humanities and Peace* vol. 22, no. 1 (2006): 58–61.
Swami Muktibodhananda (Ed.). *Hatha Yoga Pradipika: Light on Hatha Yoga*. Munger, India: Yoga Publications Trust, 2012.
Szalavitz, M. "Q&A: Jon Kabat-Zinn Talks About Bringing Mindfulness Meditation to Medicine." *TIME*. 11 January 2012. Online: http://healthland.time.com/2012/01/11/mind-reading-jon-kabat-zinn-talks-about-bringing-mindfulness-meditation-to-medicine/.
Szekeres, R.A. and Wertheim, E.H. "Evaluation of *Vipassana* Meditation Course Effects on Subjective Stress, Well-being, Self-kindness and Mindfulness in a Community Sample: Post-course and 6-month Outcomes." *Stress & Health: Journal of the International Society for the Investigation of Stress* 31 (2015): 373–381.
Tang, Y., Hölzel, B.K., and Posner, M.I. "Traits and States in Mindfulness Meditation." *Nature Reviews. Neuroscience* vol. 17, no. 1 (2016): 59.
Tangney, J.P., Dobbins, A.E., Stuewig, J.B. and Schrader, S.W. "Is There a Dark Side to Mindfulness? Relation of Mindfulness to Criminogenic Cognitions." *Personality and Social Psychology Bulletin* vol. 43, no. 10 (2017): 1415–1426.

Tart, C.T. "States of Consciousness and State-Specific Sciences." *Science* 176 (1972): 1203–1210.
Tart, C.T. "Accessing State-Specific Transpersonal Knowledge: Inducing Altered States." *The Journal of Transpersonal Psychology* vol. 40, no. 2 (2008): 137–154.
Taves, A. *Religious Experience Reconsidered*. Princeton, NJ: Princeton University Press, 2009.
Taylor, C. *Sources of the Self: The Making of the Modern Identity*. Cambridge, UK: Cambridge University Press, 1989.
The Hawn Foundation, website online: https://mindup.org/thehawnfoundation/.
Thera, S. *The Way of Mindfulness: The Satipatthana Sutta and Its Commentary*. Kandy, Sri Lanka: Buddhist Publication Society, 1998.
Thompson, E. "Looping Effects and the Cognitive Science of Mindfulness." In D.L. McMahan and E. Braun (eds) *Meditation, Buddhism, and Science*. New York, NY: Oxford University Press, 2017.
Thurman, R.A.F. and Gray, D.B. "Tsongkhapa on the Integration of Quiescence and Insight Meditation." In J. Shear (ed) *The Experience of Meditation: Experts Introduce the Major Traditions*. St. Paul, MN: Paragon House, 2006.
Tlalka, S. "Meditation is Mental Fitness—If You Do It This Way." *Mindful*. 2018. Online: https://www.mindful.org/meditation-mental-fitness-way/
Transcendental Meditation Australia, website online: https://tm.org.au/benefits-of-meditation.
Treleavan, D. "Meditation, Trauma and Contemplative Dissociation." *Somatics* vol. 16, no. 2 (2010): 20–22.
Treleaven, D.A. "Meditation and Trauma: A Hermeneutic Study of Somatic Experiencing and the Western Vipassana Movement." Unpublished PhD Dissertation. California Institute of Integral Studies, 2012.
Treleaven, D.A. *Trauma-Sensitive Mindfulness: Practices for Safe and Transformative Healing*. New York, NY: W.W. Norton & Company, 2018.
Triandis, H.C. "The Self and Social Behaviour in Differing Cultural Contexts." *Psychological Review* vol. 96, no. 3 (1989): 506–520.
Trungpa, C. *The Myth of Freedom and the Way of Meditation*. Boston, MA: Shambhala, 1976.
Van Dam, N.T., van Vugt, M.K., Vago, D.R., Schmalzl, L., Saron, C.D., Olendzki, A., Meissner, T. et al. "Mind the Hype: A Critical Evaluation and Prescriptive Agenda for Research on Mindfulness and Meditation." *Perspectives on Psychological Science* vol. 13, no. 1 (2018): 36–61.
Van de Wetering, J. *Afterzen: Experiences of a Zen Student Out on His Ear*. New York, NY: Thomas Dunne, 1999.

VanderKooi, L. "Buddhist Teachers' Experience with Extreme Mental States in Western Meditators." *The Journal of Transpersonal Psychology* vol. 29, no. 1 (1997): 31–46.

Veidlinger, D. *From Indra's Net to Internet: Communication, Technology, and the Evolution of Buddhist Ideas.* Honolulu, HI: University of Hawai'i Press, 2018.

Vendel, C. "'She Didn't Know What Was Real': Did 10-day Meditation Retreat Trigger Woman's Suicide?" *Penn Live*. 29 June 2017. Online: http://www.pennlive.com/news/2017/06/york_county_suicide_megan_vogt.html.

Vieten, C., Scammell, S., Pierce, A., Pilato, R., Ammondson, I., Pargament, K.I. and Lukoff, D. "Competencies for Psychologists in the Domains of Religion and Spirituality." *Spirituality in Clinical Practice* vol. 3, no. 2 (2016): 92–114.

Vieten, C., Scammell, S., Pilato, R., Ammondson, I., Pargament, K.I. and Lukoff, D. "Spiritual and Religious Competencies for Psychologists." *Psychology of Religion and Spirituality* vol. 5, no. 3 (2013): 129–144.

Vipassana Meditation as taught by S.N. Goenka, website online: https://www.dhamma.org/en/about/qanda.

Walach, H. *Secular Spirituality: The Next Step Towards Enlightenment.* London: Springer, 2015.

Wallace, A. "The Buddhist Science of Human Flourishing." In J. Kabat-Zinn and R.J. Davidson (eds) *The Mind's Own Physician: A Scientific Dialogue with the Dalai Lama on the Healing Power of Meditation.* Mind & Life Institute, VA: New Harbinger Publications, 2011.

Walsh, R. and Shapiro, S.L. "The Meeting of Meditative Disciplines and Western Psychology: A Mutually Enriching Dialogue." *American Psychologist* vol. 61, no. 3 (2006): 227–239.

Ward, S.J.A. *Global Media Ethics: Problems and Perspectives.* West Sussex, UK: John Wiley & Sons, 2013.

Waters, L. "Why Meditation Should be Taught in Schools." *The Conversation*. 30 June 2015. Online: https://theconversation.com/why-meditation-should-be-taught-in-schools-42755.

Welwood, J. *Toward a Psychology of Awakening: Buddhism, Psychotherapy, and the Path of Personal and Spiritual Transformation.* Boston and London: Shambhala, 2000.

Wenger, M.A., Bauchi, B.K. and Anand, B.K. "Experiments in India on 'Voluntary' Control of the Heart and Pulse." *Circulation* vol. 24, no. 6 (1961): 1319–1325.

Wexler, A. "The Social Context of 'Do-It-Yourself' Brain Stimulation: Neurohackers, Biohackers, and Lifehackers." *Frontiers in Human Neuroscience* 11, (2017): 224.

Wieczner, J. "Meditation Has Become a Billion-dollar Business." *Fortune*. 12 March 2016. Online: http://fortune.com/2016/03/12/meditation-mindfulness-apps/.

Wilber, K. "The Spectrum of Pathologies," in R. Walsh and F. Vaughan (eds) *Paths Beyond Ego: The Transpersonal Vision*. New York, NY: Tarcher/Penguin, 1993.

Wilber, K. *Up from Eden*. Wheaton, IL: Quest Books, 1996.

Wilks, J. "Secular Mindfulness: Potential and Pitfalls." *Insight Journal*. Barre Center for Buddhist Studies, 2014. Online: https://www.bcbsdharma.org/article/secular-mindfulness-potential-pitfalls/.

Williamson, L. *Transcendent in America: Hindu-Inspired Meditation Movements as New Religion*. New York, NY: New York University Press, 2010.

Wilson, B.M., Mickes, L., Stolarz-Fantino, S., Evrard, M. and Fantino, E. "Increased False-Memory Susceptibility After Mindfulness Meditation." *Psychological Science* vol. 26, no. 10 (2015): 1567–1573.

Wilson, J. *Mindful America: The Mutual Transformation of Buddhist Meditation and American Culture*. New York, NY: Oxford University Press, 2014.

Wilson, J. "Selling Mindfulness: Commodity Lineages and the Marketing of Mindful Products." In R.E. Purser, D. Forbes and A. Burke (eds) *Handbook of Mindfulness: Culture, Context and Social Engagement*. Cham, Switzerland: Springer International Publishing, 2016.

Wortham, J. "You, Only Better." *The New York Times Magazine*. 10 November 2015. Online: https://www.nytimes.com/2015/11/15/magazine/you-only-better.html?_r=1.

Yorston, G. "Mania Precipitated by Meditation: A Case Report and Literature Review." *Mental Health, Religion and Culture* vol. 4, no. 2 (2001): 209–213.

Young, S. "Enlightenment, DP/DR & Falling into the Pit of the Void." *YouTube*. 2009. Online: https://www.youtube.com/watch?v=9zIKQCwDXsA.

INDEX

abandonment depression, 24, 26
acceptance and commitment therapy (ACT), 19, 65
ACT. *See* acceptance and commitment therapy
Adams, S., 107
adverse effects (AEs), 32
AEs. *See* adverse effects
Aguirre, C., 113
Ahmed, S., 104, 119
Aleksander, I., 109
Altemeyer, B., 111
altered states of consciousness (ASC), 88
  dealing with, 94
Amar, S., 37, 95
Amihai, I., 51
Ammondson, I., 90, 125
Anand, B. K., 17
Annane, D. W., 16
anxiety, relaxation-induced, 51
Arat, A., 65, 127
Arheart, K. L., 16

Arndt, J., 58
art of living, 64
ASC. *See* altered states of consciousness
Asian meditation teachers, 54
Assagioli, R., 24
Astin, J. A., 45
awareness
  choiceless, 65
  enhancing present moment, 74
Awasthi, B., 2, 98

Bacher, P. G., 59
Baden, D., 58
Baer, R., 87, 95
Barker, K. K., 45
Barnes, A., 104
Bauchi, B. K., 17
Benedict, A. L., 99
Benson, H. I., 18, 49, 71, 107
Berger, Z., 22
Berry, D. R., 47
blocks, unconscious, 45
Boals, G. F., 50

Bogart, G., 18, 47, 53
Borup, J., 109
Borysenko, J. Z., 18, 71
bounded reality, 118
Bradwejn, J., 59
brain hygiene, 103
Brand, R. A., 62
Brasington, L., 87
Braun, E., 22, 67
Brinson, S., 36
Britton, W. B., 32, 38, 39, 48, 51, 56, 57, 58–59, 60, 126, 127
Bronn, G., 89
Brown, K. W., 47, 83, 111
Buddhism, 6
    Buddhist-derived meditation techniques, 20
    Buddhist manuals, 80
    enlightenment, 7–8
    gaining insight into nature of emptiness and non-self, 29
    ideal meditation teacher, 91
    meditation, 6
    philosophy, 7
    primordial wisdom, 8
    as scientist-philosopher, 74, 75
    traditions, 6
    as type of science, 74
    Visuddhimagga, 80
Buddhist
    concentration practices, 2
    cosmology, 69, 70
    dark night, 22–23, 28
    Modernism, 23
    Postmodernism, 23
    sympathizers, 61, 74
Burger, C., 62
Burrows, L., 37, 60, 95

Cahn, B. R., 51
Cairo, A. H., 47
Campbell, L., 104
Carlson, L. E., 45
Carrette, J. R., 111
Cartwright, T., 36, 56, 60
Castillo, R. J., 30
Cayton, A., 82

CBT. *See* Cognitive Behaviour Therapy
Chawla, N., 36, 50
Cheetah House, 39
choiceless awareness, 65
Cho, J., 103
chronic Dark Nighter, 27
churnalism, 115. *See also* meditation and media
Coe, J. H., 23
Cognitive Behaviour Therapy (CBT), 33
cognitive psychology, 47
Colgan, P., 109
Collins, S., 126
communication, scientist-journalist, 105–109
Compson, J., 36, 50
concentration
    practices, 2
    training, morality and, 85
consciousness, states of, 88
contemplative
    development, 46
    dissociation, 36
contemporary therapeutic meditation practices, 52
conventional
    development, 46
    suffering, 100
Cooper, D. J., 32, 59, 60
Creswell, J. D., 47
criminal thinking, 37
Culadasa, 86–87
cultism, 122
Cusack, C. M., 11, 109

Dalai Lama, 15
dark night, 25, 26, 32
dark night in Buddhist postmodernism, 23
dukkha nanas, 25–28
insight gone wrong, 28–32
Dark Night of the Soul, 22, 23–25. *See also* meditation adverse effects
    abandonment depression, 24
    divine homesickness, 24
    La Noche Oscura del Alma, 23
    spiritual emergence, 24

transpersonal dark night, 24–25
transpersonal psychology paradigm, 24
Dark Night Project, 38–41. *See also* meditation adverse effects
Cheetah House, 39
dark side, denial of, 117–119
Davidson, R. J., 13
Davis, J. H., 8, 51, 73
DBT. *See* dialectical behaviour therapy
de-contextualisation, 66. *See also* secular meditation
　Buddhist ideas in scientific framework, 70–71
　democratised meditation techniques, 68
　privileging of meditation, 69
　sanitised meditation, 70
　Six Patterns of Stress, 69
　Western views of Zen, 69
de Martino, R., 45
democratised meditation techniques, 68
depersonalisation and derealisation disorder (DP/DR), 29–30, 35, 93
depression, abandonment, 24, 26
Dharmamitra, 81
Dharma Overground, 26
Diagnostic and Statistical Manual of Mental Disorders, Fifth Edition (DSM-V), 30
dialectical behaviour therapy (DBT), 20
Didonna, F., 99
Dissanayaka, N., 104
dissociation, contemplative, 36
dissociative symptoms, 35
divine homesickness, 24
Dobbins, A. E., 37
Dobkin, P. L., 37, 95
Dombrowski, D. A., 23
Donovan, S., 9, 43
Dorjee, D., 20
double identity, 106
Dowdall, M., 59
DP/DR. *See* depersonalisation and derealisation disorder

Drougge, P., 105, 111
Dryden, W., 45, 46
DSM-V. See *Diagnostic and Statistical Manual of Mental Disorders, Fifth Edition*
Dubied, A., 110
Duchemin, A. M., 16
dukkha nanas, 25. *See also* meditation adverse effects
　Buddhist manuals, 25
　chronic Dark Nighter, 27
　cycles, 27
　dark night, 25, 26
　Dharma Overground, 26
　mystical peak experiences, 26
　psychological distress and dark night, 28
　off the cushion meditation, 28
Dulaney, M., 109
Dunne, J. D., 13
Dusek, J. A., 107

Eastern spiritual leaders, 9, 11
Edelglass, W., 104
Edginton, T., 36, 56, 60
EEG. *See* electroencephalographic
Eklöf, J., 105–109
electroencephalographic (EEG), 18
emergency, spiritual, 89–90
Emerson, G. B., 62
emptiness
　falling into, 30
　and non-self, 29
Engler, J., 46, 48, 55
enlightenment, 7–8, 73
　awareness, 45
　contemplative development, 46
　conventional development, 46
　issues of self and non-self, 52–56
　meditation as panacea, 44–49
　meditation as therapy, 43–44
　meditation research methods, 59–62
　mourning loss of self, 56–59
　narrative identity theory, 58
　positive psychology, 47
　relaxation response, 49–52

sophisticated psychological
    capacities, 47
  spiritual bypassing, 48
  suffering, 53–54
  to symptom relief and personal
    transformation, 43
  the farther reaches of human
    nature, 46
  unconscious, 45
  Wilber developmental model, 46
epileptogenesis, 37
Epstein, M., 46, 82, 86, 92, 97, 98
Exline, J. J., 124, 125

facing the shadow, 117
  bounded reality, 118
  denial of dark side, 117–119
  future, 123–129
  non-self, 126
  self-sealing group/system, 118
  spiritual bypassing, 119–123
  spiritually avoidant care, 125
  spiritual practices, 118
  true-self, 126
falling
  into emptiness, 30
  into void, 29, 30
Fallot, R. D., 90
fantasies, waking, 34
Farias, M., 48, 50, 108
Feuerstein, G., 3, 84, 85
Fields, R., 44
Fisher, N. E., 32, 59, 60
Fleming, L. E., 16
Foster, D., 108
Freedman, B., 45
French, A. P., 34
Fricchione, G., 47
Fromm, E., 45
Fulton, C. L., 47

Gander, K., 109
Gelles, D., 16, 111
Germer, C. K., 99
Gethin, R., 6, 126
Gleig, A., 22, 23, 25, 55, 64, 116

Goenka, S. N., 74
Goldberg, P., 11, 12, 19, 21, 109
Goldman, R. E., 51
Goldstein, 55
Goleman, D., 46, 98
Goodman, R. J., 47
Gould, N. F., 22
Goyal, M., 22
Grabovac, A., 56
Gray, D. B., 7
Gray, J. R., 107
Greene, E., 80
Green, J. D., 47
Gregoire, C., 17
Greve, D. N., 107
Greyson, B., 83, 84, 98
Grodin, M. A., 99
Grof, C., 24, 89
Grof, S., 24, 89

Habermas, J., 64
Hale, M., 21, 65, 127
halo effect, 110
Hanh, T. N., 11, 15
Hanitzsch, T., 110
Harris, D., 48
Harvey, M., 110
Hatha Yoga, 2
Hawn Foundation, The, 109
Hayes, S. C., 72
Heckman, J. D., 62
Hergovich, A., 62
Heuman, L., 107–108
Hickey, W. S., 9, 65, 85
Hinduism, 3
  concepts of gods into language
    of science, 70
  goal of Hindu meditation, 5
  philosophy, 3
  scriptures, 3, 4
  Tantric Hinduism, 12
  Vedic religious symbolism, 4
  worldview, 5
  yoga, 4
Hoffman, S. J., 110
Hölzel, B. K., 8

homesickness, divine, 24
humanistic psychotherapists, 45–46
Humes, C. A., 70, 75, 76
Hunter, K. M., 61
Huntington Jr., C. W., 54, 55
Hyland, T., 21

identity
  double, 106
  narrative, 58
IMS. *See* Insight Meditation Society;
    International Meditation
    Society
Ingalls, E., 34
Ingram, D. M., 21, 26, 27
insight gone wrong, 28. *See also*
    meditation adverse effects
  DP/DR, 29–30
  falling in void, 29, 30
  falling into emptiness, 30
  meditation sickness, 30–31
  voidness, 31
Insight Meditation Society (IMS), 14, 64
International Meditation Society (IMS),
    35
International Society for Krishna
    Consciousness (ISKCON), 11
Iny, L., 59
Irving, J. A., 37, 95
ISKCON. *See* International Society for
    Krishna Consciousness
Ivtzan, I., 108

Jaeger, S., 6
Jones, J. W., 124, 125
Josipovic, Z., 20
Jung, C. G., 117
Jyotirmayananda, 4

Kabat-Zinn, J., 13, 15, 20, 70–71, 75, 76,
    122
Kachan, D., 16
Kaplan, D., 104
Kapleau, P., 81
Katsura, S., 31, 32
Kelsey-Sugg, A., 103

Kennedy, R. B., 61
Kerr, C. E., 107
King, R., 111
Klatt, M., 16
Klipper, M. Z., 49
Klostermaier, K. K., 3, 4
Knapton, S., 104
knowledge, state specific, 73
Koneru Ramakrishna Rao, 6
Korean Son tradition, 67
Kornfield, J. M., 14, 25–28, 55, 60,
    77, 89
Kozhevnikov, M., 20, 51
Kripal, J. J., 18, 48
Krishna, G., 83
Kuijpers, H., 61
kundalini, 83
  crisis, 22, 83, 98
Kunze, S., 6
Kutz, I., 18, 71
Kuyken, W., 87, 95

Lalich, J., 118
Lam, K., 65
La Noche Oscura del Alma, 23
Lauder, J., 114
Lauricella, S., 97, 102, 103, 111
Lazar, S. W., 107
Lazarus, A., 33, 43, 51, 129
lectio divina, 2
Lee, D. J., 16
Leopold, S. S., 62
Lindahl, J. R., 32, 38, 51, 56, 57, 58–59,
    60, 126, 127
Lomas, T., 36, 56, 60
Lopez Jr, D. S., 61, 73
loss of self, 56–59
Louchakova, O., 20
Luberto, C., 47
Lu, F., 61, 89
Lukoff, D., 61, 89, 90, 125
lung, 82–83
Lustyk, M. K. B., 36, 50
Lutkajtis, A., 114
Lutz, A., 13
Lynch, G., 101

magnetic resonance imaging (MRI), 105
Mahan, J. H., 115, 116
Maharishi Mahesh Yogi, 104
Mahesh Yogi, 70, 75–76
Mahoney, A., 124, 125
makyo, 81
Mancini, L., 99
Marlatt, A. G., 36, 50
Maron, D. D., 22
Maslow, A., 46
Mastering the Core Teachings of the Buddha (MCTB), 26
Masters, R. A., 48, 119–120, 121, 122
Mayne, T. J., 51
MBCT. *See* mindfulness-based cognitive therapy
MB-Eat. *See* mindfulness-based eating awareness training
MBIs. *See* mindfulness-based interventions
MBRP. *See* mindfulness-based relapse prevention
MBSR. *See* mindfulness-based stress reduction
McAdams, D. P., 58
Mcclure, L. A., 16
Mcgarvey, M., 107
McIlwain, D., 89
McLaren, K., 118
McLean, K. C., 58
McMahan, D. L., 22, 61, 63, 66, 67
MCTB. *See Mastering the Core Teachings of the Buddha*
meaning transfer, 110. *See also* meditation and media
meditation, 1, 43, 111–115. *See also vipassana* meditation
  approaches to, 2
  Asian teachers, 54
  backlash, 21–23
  Buddhist approaches to, 6–8
  clinical, 17–20
  combined with mysticism, 34
  democratised, 68
  as detachable technique, 65–66
  experiences, 82
  goal of religious, 44
  Hindu approaches to, 3–6
  mainstream, 9–17
  in mainstream media, 101–103
  metaphorical map for practice, 95
  mindfulness, 13–17, 51, 76, 95–96
  negative effects related to, 22
  open monitoring practice, 13
  as panacea, 44–49
  permeated research, 71–72
  privileging of, 69
  in psychotherapy, 17
  relaxation view of, 51
  religious, 64, 65
  research, 32–38, 59–62
  retreat participants, 35–36
  for sale consequences, 113
  sanitised, 70
  scientific research on, 22
  secular, 21
  sickness, 30–31, 82
  teaching without preparation, 85
  techniques, 2
  off the cushion, 28
  traditional, 65, 125
  transcendental, 11–12
  transpersonal psychology, 18
  tropes, 103–105
  in West, 9, 43–44
meditation adverse effects, 21
  Britton's work on, 38–41
  Buddhist dark night, 22–23
  contemplative dissociation, 36
  criminal thinking, 37
  Dark Night of the Soul, 23–25
  Dark Night Project, 38–41
  depersonalisation and derealisation, 35
  dissociative symptoms, 35
  dukkha nanas, 25–28
  insight gone wrong, 28–32
  meditation backlash, 21–23
  meditation research, 32–38
  meditation retreat participants, 35–36
  and mysticism, 34

re-experiencing of trauma, 36
secular meditation, 21
tranquil meditator, 104
waking fantasies, 34
Western meditation-based convert Buddhist lineages, 22
meditation and media, 101
celebrity gurus and celebrity meditators, 109–111
double identity, 106
halo effect, 110
in mainstream media, 101–103
meaning transfer, 110
meditation for sale, 111–115
meditation tropes, 103–105
mental hygiene, 103
news stories, 101–103
portrayal, 115–116
scientist-journalist communication, 105–109
self-improvement, 112
sensationalistic reporting, 108
meditation and religion, 79
adverse effects, 79–84
conventional suffering, 100
individual differences and psychopathology, 97–100
kundalini crisis, 83, 98
lung, 82–83
makyo, 81
and marginalising religious context, 66–71
meditation-related ASCs, 88–89
morality and concentration training, 85
nyams, 82
preparation, 84–87
proponents of meditation techniques, 79
psychological problems, 86
secular meditation, 112
spiritual emergency, 89–90
spiritual hygiene, 103
spiritual marketplace, 111
states of consciousness, 88
supportive context, 88–91

teacher and technique, 91–97
teaching meditation without preparation, 85
Theravada Buddhism, 80, 85
Western secular frameworks, 88
Zen Buddhism, 81
Zen sickness, 82
meditation teacher, 91, 109
contemporary Buddhist teachers, 92, 93
metaphorical map for practice, 95
mindfulness meditation teacher training, 95–96
roles of, 91
strategies to deal with altered states, 94
vipassana meditators, 93
meditative attainments, 52
meditator, tranquil, 104
Mehta, A., 16
Meissner, T., 105, 107, 108
Melbourne Academic Mindfulness Interest Group, 95
mental hygiene, 103
Michaelson, J., 17
mindfulness, 2, 13, 72, 102. *See also* meditation
-based stress reduction, 15
concentration on object, 15
goal of meditation, 51
Hanh, 15
key sources of teaching, 13–14
media reporting on, 16–17
meditation, 76
practice, 15
in secular settings, 16
teacher training, 95–96
vipassana course, 14
mindfulness-based cognitive therapy (MBCT), 19
mindfulness-based eating awareness training (MB-Eat), 20
mindfulness-based interventions (MBIs), 37
mindfulness-based relapse prevention (MBRP), 20

mindfulness-based stress reduction (MBSR), 15, 49, 99
Mitchell, J. P., 101
Mitchell, S., 104, 105
modern Western secular meditation, 44
Moore, C. I., 107
morality and concentration training, 85
Motes, M. A., 20
MRI. *See* magnetic resonance imaging
Murphy, M., 9, 43
mysticism and meditation, 34

Nargajuna, 31
narrative identity theory, 58
Nelson, L. W., 82, 91
Neo-Freudian psychoanalysts, 18
neural deficits, 72
neuroplasticity, 113
Nickerson, R. S., 62
Nolan, R. S., 36, 50
non-self, 52, 126
    emptiness and, 29
    realisation of, 58
nyams, 82

off the cushion meditation, 28
Ohanian, R., 110
Olano, H., 16
Olendzki, A., 105, 107, 108
Oliver, P., 10
Otis, L. S., 34–35, 47
Ozawa-de Silva, B., 20

Paine, J., 91
Paranjpe, A. C., 17
Pargament, K. I., 90, 124, 125
Park, E., 47
Parsons, W. B., 9, 18, 47, 48, 58, 106
Paterniti, M., 104
Payne, R. K., 112
Perls, F., 45
permeated meditation research, 71–72
Pflugshaupt, A., 103
philosophy
    Hinduism, 3
    spiritual beliefs and, 122–123

Philpotts, L., 47
Pickert, K., 17
Pierce, A., 90
Pilato, R., 90, 125
pit of the void, 29, 30
positive psychology, 47
Posner, M. I., 8
post-traumatic stress disorder (PTSD), 83
Prebish, C. S., 77
primordial wisdom, 8
Pringle, G., 109
Pritchard, S. M., 56, 60, 93–94
Provenzano, R., 89
psychoanalysis, 46
psychological suffering, 54
psychology
    aspects of, 74
    cognitive, 47
    positive, 47
    transpersonal, 18, 46
    transpersonal paradigm, 24
psychotherapeutic processes, 47
PTSD. *See* post-traumatic stress disorder
Purser, R. E., 22, 73, 74

Quaglia, J. T., 47
Quinn, B. T., 107

Raghavendra, B. R., 4
Rapgay, L., 82
Rauch, S. L., 107
reality, bounded, 118
re-contextualisation, 74–77
reductionism, 72
relaxation
    -induced anxiety, 51
    response, 49–52
    techniques, 49
    view of meditation, 51
religious meditation, 64, 65
Remski, M. D., 118
research, meditation, 32–38
Richmond, L., 31, 93
Ridge, D., 36, 56, 60

INDEX   159

Rocha, T., 38, 39
Rosch, E., 8, 53, 79
Rosen, R. K., 32, 59, 60
Rosenthal, N. E., 109
Rosenthal, R., 62
Routledge, C., 58
Rowland-Seymour, A., 22
Rusby, J., 111
Ryan, R. M., 47

Samuel, G., 52, 82
Sannella, L., 83
Santorelli, S., 100
Saron, C. D., 105, 107, 108
Scammell, S., 90, 125
Schmalzl, L., 105, 107, 108
Schmid, A. C., 34
Schott, R., 62
Schrader, S. W., 37
Schwartz, S. Y., 103
Science of Creative Intelligence, 76
scientist-journalist communication, 105–109
secularism, 63
   modern West secularism, 64
secular meditation, 21, 63–65, 112
   acceptance and commitment therapy, 65
   art of living, 64
   choiceless awareness, 65
   de-contextualisation, 66–71
   enhancing awareness in present moment, 74
   enlightenment, 73
   MBSR, 65
   meditation as detachable technique, 65–66
   permeated meditation research, 71–72
   re-contextualisation, 74–77
   reductionism, 72
   and religious meditation, 64
   Science of Creative Intelligence, 76
   simplification, 71–74
   state specific knowledge, 73

   in therapy, 34
   transcendent sense of self, 65
Sedikides, C., 58
Sedlmeier, P., 5, 6, 74, 98
Seiden, D. Y., 65
self
   -improvement, 112
   loss of, 56–59
   and non-self issues, 52–56
   -realisation, 52
   -sealing group, 118
   sense of, 56
   six discrete changes in, 56
   transcendent sense of, 65
   true-self, 126
Seppälä, E. M., 103
shadow, facing the. *See* facing the shadow
Shafranske, E. P., 124, 125
Shapiro, D. H., 19, 35, 49
Shapiro, S. L., 45, 47, 88
Sharf, R. H., 13, 30, 65, 67, 68, 87, 127
Sharma, R., 22
Sheng-yen, 93
Shenk, C., 72
Shihab, H. M., 22
Shinday, N., 47
Shunsky, S., 104
Sibinga, E. M. S., 22
Siderits, M, 31, 32
Siegel, A., 72, 128
simplification, 71–74
SIMS. *See* Students International Meditation Society
Singh, N. N., 74
Singh, P., 4
Singh, S., 22
Singleton, M., 4
Six Patterns of Stress, 69
Slagter, H. A., 13
Sleicher, D., 22
Smith, J. C., 44
Song, R., 47
sophisticated psychological capacities, 47
Sperry, L., 91

Spirit Rock, 64
spiritual
    Eastern leaders, 9, 11
    emergency, 22, 89–90
    gullibility, 122
    gurus, 109
    hygiene, 103
    marketplace, 111
    practices, 118
spiritual bypassing, 48, 119
    collective spiritual bypassing, 120
    as lack of critical thinking, 122
    magical thinking, 122
    negative emotions, 120
    privileging transcendence, 121
    psychotherapy, 121
    spiritual beliefs and philosophies, 122–123
spirituality, 66
    avoidant care, 125
SR & RP. *See* Stress Reduction and Relaxation Program
Srinivas, K., 5, 74, 98
Stahl, A., 16
Stanley, S., 74
state specific knowledge, 73
Steinberg. B., 16
Stevens, R., 111
Still, A., 45, 46
Stress Reduction and Relaxation Program (SR & RP), 15. *See also* mindfulness-based stress reduction
Stress, Six Patterns of, 69
Strhan, A., 101
Students International Meditation Society (SIMS), 35, 47
Stuewig, J. B., 37
suffering, 53
    conventional, 100
    psychological, 54
Suler, J., 48
Sun, J., 16, 102
Suzuki, D. T., 45
Sydnor, A., 36
sympathizers, 61, 74

Szalavitz, M., 66
Szekeres, R. A., 14

Tan, C., 110
Tangney, J. P., 37
Tang, Y., 8
Tannenbaum, S. L., 16
Tantric Hinduism, 12
Tart, C. T., 72, 88
Taves, A., 2
Taylor, C., 1
Theosophical Society, 109
Theravada
    Buddhism, 80, 85
    monks, 67
thinking, criminal, 37
Thompson, E., 73
Thurman, R. A. F., 7
Tirumalai Krishnamacharya, 17
Tlalka, S., 112
TM. *See* Transcendental Meditation
traditional meditation, 65
tranquil meditator, 104
Transcendental Meditation (TM), 2, 11, 33, 65, 102. *See also* meditation
    concentration on specific object, 15
    technique, 64
    TM-Sidhi technique, 12
transcendent sense of self, 65
transpersonal psychology, 18, 46
trauma re-experienced, 36
trauma-related unpleasant sensations, 120
Treadway, M. T., 107
Treleavan, D. A., 36, 61, 64, 99, 120
Triandis, H. C., 53
true-self, 126
Trungpa, C., 70
Tuinier, S., 61
Turner, R., 61, 89

unconscious, 45
unpleasant trauma-related sensations, 120
Upanishadic traditions. *See* Hinduism

Vago, D. R., 8, 73, 105, 107, 108
Van Dam, N. T., 105, 107, 108
van der Heijden, F., 61
VanderKooi, L., 80, 94
Van de Wetering, J., 92
van Vugt, M. K., 105, 107, 108
Varieties of Contemplative Experience (VOCE), 40. *See also* Dark Night Project
Vedic religious symbolism, 4
Veidlinger, D., 115, 116
Vendel, C., 97
Verhoeven, W., 61
Vieten, C., 90, 125
Vigyan Bhairav Tantra, 2
vipassana meditation, 2, 64, 68, 75. *See also* meditation
  non-self experiences in, 55
vipassana meditators, 93
VOCE. *See* Varieties of Contemplative Experience
voidness, 31, 93
void, pit of, 29, 30

waking fantasies, 34
Walach, H., 66
Wallace, A., 95
Walsh, R. N., 19, 45, 47, 49, 88
Ward, S. J. A., 115
Warme, W. J., 62
Wasserman, R. H., 107
Waters, L., 16
Welwood, J., 119, 120, 124
Wenger, M. A., 17
Wertheim, E. H., 14
Western
  meditation-based convert Buddhist lineages, 22
  psychology, 100
  psychotherapy, 121
  teachers, 76, 69
  views of Zen, 69
Western Vipassana Meditation (WVM), 64–65
Wexler, A., 112
Wieczner, J., 16
Wikholm, C., 48, 50, 108
Wilber, K., 24
  developmental model, 46
Wildschut, T., 58
Wilks, J., 21
Williamson, L., 11, 12
Wilson, J., 9, 12, 13, 15, 16, 61, 69, 76, 106, 109, 114
wisdom, primordial, 8
Wolf, F. M., 62
World Plan Executive Council (WPEC), 35
Wortham, J., 113
WPEC. *See* World Plan Executive Council
WVM. *See* Western Vipassana Meditation

Yang, X., 16
Yeh, G., 47
yoga, 4. *See also* meditation
Yorston, G., 61
Young, S., 28, 93

Zajac, B., 103
Zen, 69
  Buddhism, 81
  meditation, 76
  sickness, 82
  Western views of, 69

www.ingramcontent.com/pod-product-compliance
Ingram Content Group UK Ltd.
Pitfield, Milton Keynes, MK11 3LW, UK
UKHW021846140426
5217IPUK00022B/1619